D1083445

THE REALM OF MUSIC

By

NICK ROSSI

Assistant Professor of Music
University of Bridgeport

CRESCENDO PUBLISHING COMPANY
BOSTON

DEDICATED TO H. K.

Library of Congress Catalog Card No. 73-81255

ISBN 0-87597-086-9

Printed in the United States of America

CONTENTS

Chapter I
MUSIC ALL AROUND US

Did you ever stop to realize that music is all around us, every day? We hear a marching band at a football game. We hear the latest rock tune on our portable radios. We hear the organ that accompanies the singing at our church or temple. We hear the soundtrack from the latest movie. Even the commercials we hear on radio and TV are accompanied by music. There may even be background music in an elevator, or in an office building, or at a restaurant we visit.

Now take a moment to think about all this music. What makes it music? What is the stuff of which it is made?

To find out the answers, why not bring one of this week's Top Ten to class and listen to it? And, as you listen, try to discover why this single is such a big hit.

When you start to answer this question, you'll probably think about two important things: the <u>beat</u> and the <u>tune</u>. It's usually one or the other — or maybe even the two together — that help us enjoy a new record and make us want to hear it again. If the beat and the tune are really good, we may even want to buy the record for our own collection.

The beat and the tune are two very important parts of all music. (The professional musicians call <u>beat</u> and <u>tune</u> the <u>rhythm</u> and <u>melody</u> of music.) Think about some of the music you like best. Almost every piece has a good beat or rhythm to it. And, each one has a tune or melody that we like to hum, sing, or whistle.

IRONSIDE

by Quincy Jones

Let's listen to some more music so that we can understand this business of rhythm and melody a little better. For our example we'll choose music Quincy Jones wrote for the television series called "Ironside."

When the writer and producers first thought of the detective story "Ironside" for a weekly TV series, they knew they wanted theme music that would be catchy and could easily be remembered. They knew that in that way people would hear the music and remember the TV show. The directors decided to ask Quincy Jones to write the theme music. Jones had already written successful scores for such movies as "The Pawn - broker" and "Mirage." The directors were convinced that Jones would do a good job on the theme music they wanted.

Quincy Jones accepted the job. As he started to work on the TV score, he realized that the beat or rhythm he decided on would be extremely important. It would need to be bold and lively if he was going to catch the attention of TV viewers and make them want to watch the show that followed. Jones knew that almost everybody likes a good, driving rock beat, and that such a rhythm would attract people's attention immediately. In the staff notation that musicians use, the rock rhythm Quincy Jones decided to use looks like this:

If you listen to the opening of "Ironside," you can hear the rhythm section with this beat.

After he had decided on the basic rhythm or beat, Jones knew he needed a good tune or melody to put over it. Especially if he was going to make this a bit of jazz-rock music. Once he had this melody in mind, he had next to decide what instrument was going to play it. He thought he would do something rather new and different. Instead of giving the melody to a sax or trumpet as in most jazz, he decided to write the melody for a solo flute! So that the dynamic level of the flute — its loudness — would be high enough to be heard over the rhythm section, Jones asked the flutist to play this melody into a microphone. In staff notation Jones' tune looks like this:

Example 1

Rhythm (beat): Rhythm is everything which pertains to the duration of the musical sound, including alternating periods of sound and silence. It is the organization of music with respect to time. It deals with stress and accentuation.

Melody (tune): Melody is a memorable succession of single musical tones having a recognizable musical shape or contour.

Quincy Jones

(March 14, 1933 -   )

As a boy, Quincy Jones learned to play the trumpet. He started his professional music career during his high school days by arranging some music for an Oscar Pettiford record album . To gain a better working knowledge of music, Jones enrolled at the Berklee School of Music in Boston where he studied jazz. He next took a job with Barclay Records in Paris so that he could study classical composition with Nadia Boulanger, the most famous twentieth - century teacher of composition.

When Quincy Jones returned to the United States, he appeared with several bands as a trumpet player. These bands included those of Lionel Hampton and Dizzy Gillespie among others. Finally Jones founded his own band.

Quincy Jones has written music for both movies and TV, and has cre-

4

ated a number of memorable tunes for several highly successful long – playing record albums.

THE   GODFATHER

by Nino Rota

Whether we are listening to rock or some romantic background music from a good movie, we soon discover that both rhythm and melody are very, very important. Proof of this can be found in the music of the title song from the 1973 Oscar-winning movie, "The Godfather."

When Albert S. Ruddy, the producer of the film, was planning the movie, he knew he wanted a title song that would be a "hit" in its own right, thus attracting people who heard it on radio or TV to come see the movie. He decided to ask an Italian-American composer named Nino Rota to write the music, as Rota had been highly successful writing theme music for Franco Zeffirelli's movie, "Romeo and Juliet."

Since his title song was to serve in the movie as a love theme, Rota decided against using a hard, rock beat. Instead he chose a rather slow, flowing four-beat rhythm to accompany his melody.

The tune itself was slow, melodic, and quite romantic:

Example 1*

Nino Rota

(December 3, 1911-   )

Nino Rota was born in Milan, Italy, and had his first composition — an oratorio — publically performed when he was eleven! At fourteen, a three act opera of his was produced in Rome.

Rota studied composition first at the St. Cecilia Academy in Rome, and then attended the Curtis Institute of Music in Philadelphia. After

finishing his training in Pennsylvania, he returned to Italy in 1937 to become a teacher. In 1950 he became the Director of the Music Academy in
Bari, Italy.

Nino Rota has composed several symphonies and sonatas in addition
to an opera for radio, and many film scores for both Italian and American
movies.

Chapter II

THE UNITED STATES:
EAST AND WEST

In addition to background music for movies and title music for television, there is another type of music. It is music that is meant just for
listening. It doesn't serve to help the story in a movie, or to attract
television viewers to watch the following program. Such music doesn't
accompany a dance; it isn't used to rouse the crowd at a football game
to cheer. It is this type of music — music for listening — to which we
shall listen next.

Why should we listen to such music? Because we find it pleasurable
and enjoyable, and because we feel better inside for having heard it .
And, as with anything for which we must put forth an effort to understand
— to learn what it is all about — we will appreciate this music for listening more when we have tried our best to understand it.

Music speaks in beautiful melodies, in catchy rhythms, in the varying qualities of tone from different instruments. Sometimes music is loud,
sometimes it is soft; sometimes it moves quickly , at other times it
moves slowly. Music is its own language. It doesn't tell stories; it
doesn't describe landscapes or country scenes.

The realm of music is a world of tone, including all the qualities of
tone such as pitch, intensity, dynamics. It is a realm of tones arranged
melodically and rhythmically. The realm of music is also a realm of
order, of form, of design. These are the elements of music.

As you listen to the compositions described in this book you will
learn to understand what the music means through its own language:
melody and rhythm (which we have already talked about), and the way
melody and rhythm are put together, the form of the music. You will discover that there are differences in the tone quality or timbre of different
instruments and voices. Melodies, you will learn, move along at varying
speeds; the musician calls this tempo. Music also has variety in its
dynamics, the degrees of softness and loudness.

We have just said that music does not tell a story; sometimes, however, a composer is inspired by a good yarn, a painting or perhaps a
poem. When this happens, he frequently names the resulting composition
after the object of his enthusiasm; it might be "Don Juan," "The Swan of
Tuonela" or "Rodeo." We call this program music, music in which the
creator uses sound to suggest a story or image.

Although the composer might have a very detailed idea in his mind of
this non-musical idea — the poem, painting or tale — he doesn't always

6

leave a written clue for the listener. Sometimes one is able to discover from the music the program the composer had in mind. At other times, it has little to do with the enjoyment of the music.

As you listen to the compositions in this chapter, you should be able to discover the program by listening to the music. Because you are already familiar with some types of music, they bring to mind different places and circumstances. Fiddles tuning in a certain way might suggest to you a square dance or a hoe-down. When a military rhythm or a martial tune is played, you might recall a marching band.

As you progress in your listening experiences, you will discover that music doesn't always have to be associated with something specific . You will learn to enjoy a melody for its own beauty, a rhythm will impress you because it is unlike any other rhythm pattern you have ever heard.

This is the language of music. It speaks to the heart and to the mind.

RODEO

by Aaron Copland

"Rodeo," or "The Courting at Burnt Ranch" (its subtitle) is a ballet based on a western story created by the famous choreographer Agnes de Mille who described it as follows:

> "Throughout the American southwest, the Saturday afternoon rodeo is a tradition. On the remote ranches, as well as in the trading centers and towns, the 'hands' get together to show off their skill in roping, riding, branding and throwing. Often, on the more isolated ranches, the rodeo is done for an audience that consists of only a handful of fellow-workers, women-folk and those nearest neighbors who can make the eighty or so mile run-over.

> "The afternoon's exhibition is usually followed by a Saturday night dance at the Ranch House."[1]

In the opening scene of the ballet, the cowboys of Burnt Ranch are gathered for their weekly rodeo. The young Cowgirl, a tomboy, becomes aware of men for the first time, for she has developed a mad crush on the Head Wrangler! In an attempt to show off for him, she gets thrown from a bucking bronco. Everybody laughs at her, including some city girls who have stopped by for the dance that will follow the rodeo. The Cowgirl's heart is broken, for the Head Wrangler goes off with the Rancher's Daughter.

That evening at the Saturday night dance, the Cowgirl, still dressed in Levis and boots, appears lonesome and neglected. Her friend, the Champion Roper, takes pity on this wallflower and shows her how to dance a few steps. Just as the lesson is progressing, she sees the Head Wrangler waltzing cheek to cheek with the Rancher's Daughter. The Cowgirl runs away in misery.

The ranch hands, who have continued to dance, stop in astonishment when the Cowgirl returns. For the first time she has put on a party dress and done her hair up with a bow. The men discover what a pretty girl she really is. The Head Wrangler now competes with the Champion Roper for her attention. She settles on the Roper, the only man that has ever shown her any attention.

In the music to accompany this ballet, composer Aaron Copland has used a number of western folk songs. One of these is an old cowboy tune, "Old Paint," that you might like to sing. Another is an old fiddler's tune, "Bonaparte's Retreat Across the Rocky Mountains."

The ballet was so successful when it was first presented at the Metropolitan Opera House in New York, the composer was asked to make an orchestral suite from it for use on concert programs. He called his suite "Four Dance Episodes from Rodeo." These four include: (1) "Buckaroo Holiday"; (2) "Corral Nocturne"; (3) "Saturday Night Waltz"; and (4) "Hoe Down."

Saturday Night Waltz

The "Saturday Night Waltz" opens with an introduction in which the string instruments sound as if they are tuning. Finally they sustain a B-flat pitch as the brass enter with a G-flat major chord.

The tempo changes to a slow waltz. The oboe plays a haunting melody that reminds one of the folk song on which it is based, "Old Paint":

Example 1*

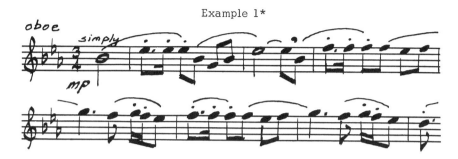

The violins repeat this beautiful melody with the oboe joining the violins in the fourth measure.

The violas play a haunting melody in answer to the violin-oboe tune.

Once again the violins and oboe play Example 1; a counter-melody in the flute is heard above it.

Eight measures of a sustained B in the woodwinds and strings lead to the middle section of the waltz. The tempo becomes slower. After a brief passage for the solo clarinet, the violas enter with a new melody:

· Example 2

The flute and clarinet carry on a duet above this long viola melody.

The tempo returns to that of the first section. After a five measure passage in which one is reminded of the "Old Paint" tune, the violins and oboe repeat the melody of Example 1. This brings the waltz to a close.

Counter-melody: A melody of secondary importance that is heard simultaneously with the principal melody.

Ternary Form: If the melody of Example 1 were lettered A, and that of Example 2 were lettered B, the use of these melodies in this movement could be outlined as A - B - A. The musician calls this a three-part or ternary form, the

* All themes from "Rodeo" : Copyright 1946 by Aaron Copland. Reprinted by permission of Aaron Copland and Boosey & Hawkes, Inc., Sole Licensees

third part being a melodic repetition of the first, although usually only half as long.

Orchestral Suite: Just as a hotel manager calls a group of separate rooms with connecting doors a <u>suite</u>, so the musician calls a group of separate movements connected by some link a <u>suite</u>. The musical link may be the use of the same melody in each movement, or it might be that all the movements are dances, or, as in the case of "Rodeo," the connecting link might be the story.

Choreographer: A person, usually a dancer, who artistically designs the movements and actions of the dancers in a ballet or modern dance.

Hoe Down

An introduction to the "Hoe Down" starts with many repetitions of Figure A from Example 3A quoted below. Then, for nine measures, the strings sound as if they are tuning; in the meantime, the brass instruments play a rhythmic figure. More repetitions of Figure A follow. An important rhythm is then introduced:

The first section of the "Hoe Down" opens with a melody played by the violins, a direct quotation — note for note — of the old fiddler's tune , "Bonyparte" (sometimes called "Bonaparte's Retreat Across the Rocky Mountains"):

Example 3A

The violins complete the tune:

Example 3B

Example 3A is repeated by the violins. The first half of Example 3B is then played by the strings; the last half is played by the woodwinds.

The entire orchestra, in a very loud passage, repeats Example 3B. Violins and clarinets play Example 3A through once more in its entirety; on an immediate repetition they get stuck on Figure A which they repeat several times.

The middle section of this three-part (ternary) form is based on a saucy little trumpet tune:

Example 4

As this tune continues, it is played in turn by the violins and the oboe. The violins repeat the melody of Example 4.

In a passage that "bridges" to the closing section, the piano and brass are heard with the rhythmic figure

which alternates with a sixteenth-note string passage.

After a dynamic climax, the rhythm of the introduction returns in the piano:

The closing section begins with Example 3A played by the violins and clarinet. Example 3B follows, started by the woodwinds and finished by the full orchestra. The melody of Example 3A is heard once more, and leads to the close of this wild hoe down.

Aaron Copland

(November 14, 1900 -   )

Aaron Copland was born in an old house in Brooklyn, New York, and lived there in the same house for the first twenty years of his life. He was ten when he first became interested in music; he was thirteen when he decided to become a musician. Because his family had experienced bad luck trying to provide music lessons for the older children in the family (they quickly lost interest), Aaron was put on his own to find a piano teacher and arrange for lessons.

Just two years after starting these lessons, Copland decided that he was going to become a composer. At nineteen he traveled to France — to Fontainebleau, a short drive south of Paris — where he enrolled at the then new American School. Three years later, after he had completed his studies, his teacher Nadia Boulanger asked him to compose a work for pipe organ and orchestra. She was an organist herself and about to tour the United States, playing the pipe organ with leading symphony orchestras.

Copland wrote the music after his return to the United States, in Milford , Pennsylvania , where he found a job playing in a hotel trio to earn money for his room and board. This new "Symphony for Orchestra and Organ" was so successful when it was played in Boston, the conductor of that orchestra asked Copland to write another work.

These early compositions of Copland were influenced by jazz. Later he turned to folk-songs for inspiration, using them first in his ballet " El Salon Mexico " in 1936. Several ballets followed that were also based on folk songs: "Billy the Kid" (1938), "Rodeo" (1942) , and "Appalachian Spring" (1944) .

Courtesy of Boosey & Hawkes.

In more recent years the composer has written a number of major orchestral works that are not programmatic.

THREE PLACES IN NEW ENGLAND

by Charles Ives

Charles Ives was a quiet, retiring insurance executive — in fact, the most successful insurance broker in New York prior to his retirement in the 1920s. His evenings were spent at home, writing music that almost no one performed during his lifetime. Much of this music, now played frequently, was inspired by America — the countryside, its holidays, its history. He has written works to commemorate Thanksgiving Day, the Fourth of July, Washington's Birthday, and many other holidays. Other compositions celebrate places that he knew and loved in his native New England.

During the years 1903 to 1914, Ives worked on his "New England Symphony," usually called "Three Places in New England." Its second movement, called "Putnam's Camp,"is one of his most interesting compositions.

Putnam's Camp

Putnam's Camp is the name of a Revolutionary War memorial. In Ives' musical composition of the same name, he has created a musical fantasy, suggesting dreams of a child who falls asleep on the hillside overlooking this camp during a Fourth of July outing. A riot of march rhythms are heard, along with bits of well-known tunes. Bands come marching from either side, the harmonies of their different tunes clashing as they pass each other. Humorously, the rhythm skips a beat as the drummer in one of the bands stumbles on a stone.

Although the musical structure is as complicated as a Chinese puzzle, its sounds closely parallel the very detailed description that Ives wrote in the musical score for "Putnam's Camp":

"Near Redding Center, Connecticut, is a small park preserved as a Revolutionary Memorial; for here General Israel Putnam's soldiers had their winter quarters in 1778-1779. Long rows of stone camp-fire places still remain to stir a child's imagination. The hardships which the soldiers endured and the agitation of a few hot-heads to break camp and march to the Hartford Assembly for relief, is part of Redding history.

"Once upon a 'Fourth of July' some time ago, so the story goes, a child went there on a picnic, held under the

auspices of the First Church and the Village Cornet Band.
Wandering away from the rest of the children past the
camp ground into the woods, he hopes to catch a glimpse
of some of the old soldiers. As he rests on the hillside of
laurel and hickories, the tunes of the band and the songs
of the children grow fainter and fainter; — when — strange
to say — over the trees on the crest of the hill he sees a
tall woman standing. She reminds him of a picture he has
of the Goddess of Liberty, — but the face is sorrowful —
she is pleading with the soldiers not to forget their
'cause' and the great sacrifices they have made for it. But
they march out of camp with fife and drum to a popular
tune of the day. Suddenly a new national note is heard.
Putnam is coming over the hills from center, — the soldiers turn back and cheer. The little boy awakes, he
hears the children's songs and runs down past the monu-
ment to 'listen to the band' and join in the games and
dances."*

The composer goes on in this written introduction to his music to ex-
plain why in a composition representing the American forces, he has used
a tune popularly known as "The British Grenadiers":

"The repertoire of national airs at the time was meagre.
Most of them were of English origin. It is a curious fact
that a tune very popular with the American soldiers was
'The British Grenadiers.' A Captain in one of Putnam's
regiments put it to words, which were sung for the first
time in 1779 at a patriotic meeting in the Congregational
Church in Redding Center; the text is both ardent and
interesting."*

If one listens carefully to the music, most of Ives' "story" can be
discovered from the music.
"Putnam's Camp" opens at a march tempo; the composer marks the
music "Quickstep time." A bold, descending scale passage for full orchestra leads to a rhythmic passage for the drums. (If you listen closely,
you can hear them miss a beat as they fall out of step for a moment!) After the percussion has established the march-nature of the movement, the
violins introduce the theme of the "Village Cornet Band":

Example 1*

Violins

* Copyright 1935 - Mercury Music, Inc. Used by permission.

In a rather lengthy passage, a syncopated version of Figure A, in which the accents do not occur in the expected places, is played many times by the violins.

The trumpets enter with "the songs of the children." A melodic fragment which suggests "Turkey in the Straw" is heard first while the trombones and tuba play a counter-melody suggestive of a Sousa march tune:

Example 2

Example 2 is followed by melodic fragments of other "songs of children": "Hail, Columbia," "Yankee Doodle" and "Oh! Susanna."

Example 3

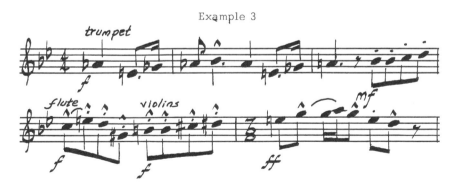

The music becomes very soft; the violins play Example 4:

Example 4

In another rather lengthy passage, the music becomes softer and softer as "the songs of the children grow fainter and fainter." Low, sustained tones for low strings preceed a sustained, very soft chord.

The tempo changes to <u>Andante animato</u> (suggestive of the "sorrowful Goddess of Liberty"). A brief, two-measure flute solo over a sustained string chord introduces Example 5. Before Example 5 is completed by the oboe, the martial rhythm of the drums is heard.

Example 5

Gradually the tempo accelerates. The French horns introduce the "march out of camp with fife and drum to a popular tune of the day" (the "British Grenadiers"):

Example 6

Soon "the little boy awakes, he hears the children's songs" — this time the old round, "Row, Row, Row Your Boat":

Example 7

trumpets, French horns

The music builds to a dynamic climax. The violins then take up Example 4 very softly.

Once again the music builds in volume. Syncopated chords for full orchestra lead to the return of the "Village Band" tune, Example 1. At the same time, other melodic fragments are heard — including the "British Grenadier" tune, Example 6. From here to the end of the movement, one hears both bands, and, from time to time, the fragments of the children's tunes.

> Syncopation : A passage or melody in which the stresses or accents fall in other than the expected places is said to be syncopated. The composer achieves this in one of several ways; by anticipation (the stress occurring earlier than expected); by suspension (the stress occurring later than expected); by an indicated stress on an unexpected beat; or, by having a rest on the beat and sound on a subdivision of the beat.

Charles Ives

(October 20, 1874-May 19, 1954)

Charles Ives was born in Danbury, Connecticut, not far from where his forebears had settled shortly after the landing of the Pilgrims. His father had been a band leader in the Union Army during the Civil War; his mother was a music teacher.

As a boy, Charles attended the outdoor camp meetings, becoming familiar at an early age with revival songs. When he was eight, his father caught him thumping out march rhythms on the piano. Music lessons were soon provided for him.

By eleven he was the regular organist for the Congregational Church in Danbury and was composing music for his father's town band to play.

After graduating from college, Ives decided that if he was to support a wife and rear a family, he had better look for work in some field other than music. He turned to insurance, a business in which he made millions of dollars during his career. Composing music became for him a hobby, a past-time; he never expected to hear much of it performed.

Since his death many of his works have become well known: more than 200 songs, several violin and piano sonatas, four symphonies, three orchestral suites, eleven volumes of chamber music, and a quantity of choral works.

Chapter III

OF TRAVEL
AND FOREIGN PLACES

In the last chapter we discovered that music is distinguished from everything else in the world by its unique quality, <u>tone</u>. It is this that appeals to us, that makes us want to listen to music. We understand music when we know the nature of a musical tone and can discover the ways in which tones may be combined. One of these ways is in a horizontal line, one after another; we call this <u>melody</u>.

We also discovered that a musical tone has pitch, duration, dynamics and timbre ("color" or characteristic quality). As you study the music in this chapter, you will develop an awareness of higher and lower pitches. You will discover that some melodies move in tones of long time value, some in tones of short duration. Most melodies move in tones of varying time value. You will learn that tones and the melodies that they form may sound relatively soft or loud, and that one and the same pitch or melody can sound differently when played by various instruments.

As an example, sing through the melody from the opening of a well-known Christmas carol:

In which part of this melody are the pitches higher and in which part are they lower? Sing it again, making every note of the same time value or duration. Does this change the very character of the melody? Also discover that if you sing this melody loudly, it sounds as though you are proclaiming "Joy to the world!" If you sing it very softly, discover how it changes the whole nature of the message: it sounds as though one is standing in awe, witnessing a miracle and saying in a hushed voice, "Joy to the world."

As a final experiment, listen to this melody sung on a neutral syllable (perhaps "ah") and then listen to it played on the piano. The difference is in the timbre or tone color. It would sound still differently if it were played by a clarinet, or a violin or by a trumpet.

In the music in this chapter, all of which is program music, the

19

composer has attempted to suggest a geographical area. Try to discover, as you listen to the music, how the composer accomplishes this through the use of melodies and the manner in which they are employed.

ESPAÑA: Rhapsody for Orchestra

by Emmanuel Chabrier

In 1882 Emmanuel Chabrier, a French composer, visited Spain. He was completely fascinated by the music he heard and the dancing he saw in that colorful country. Enthusiastically he wrote home to a friend:

> "In a month I must leave this adorable Spain, and say goodbye to the Spaniard! I have not truly seen a really ugly woman since I have been in Andalusia; add to that beauty the inevitable fan, the flower and the comb in the hair, and the shawl of Chinese cloth embroidered in flowers.

> "Every evening we go to the cafe-concerts where the malagueñas, the soledas and the sapateados are sung. Then the dances! At Malaga the dancing became intense! I have no need to tell you that I have noted down many things."

Among the things that Chabrier "noted down" were a number of authentic Spanish tunes and melodies. After returning to his home in Paris the composer used six of these melodies, plus one original tune (Example 7 below) in an orchestral work which he called "España." Rather than cast these melodies in a strict form (for example, the ternary form), he organized the melodies loosely, one after another, in what he called a rhapsody. To the poet, a rhapsody means "an exalted or exaggerated expression of enthusiasm, an epic poem." It was in this sense of exaltation — almost exaggeration — of enthusiasm with Spanish melodies and rhythms, that Chabrier wrote an "epic" piece of orchestral music.

"España" is based chiefly on two Spanish dances, both in triple meter (three beats or pulses in a measure). One of these dances is the jota, a dance from northern Spain. It is always sung by the dancers who accompany themselves with guitars and castanets, playing as they dance. The rhythm of the jota is fiery and forceful:

The other rhythm which the composer used was from Malaga and named after that city, the malagueña. Although accompanied by castanets also,

it is a slower, dreamier, almost romantic dance. The rhythm of the malagueña is:

"España" opens with a rhythmic introduction played by the strings pizzicato (plucked rather than bowed) and the castanets.

The malagueña theme is introduced by the bassoons and muted trumpet:

Example 1

Example 1 is repeated by the French horns to the accompaniment of the harp, castanets and triangle.

A more lyric (song-like) theme is played by the bassoons, horns and cellos:

Example 2

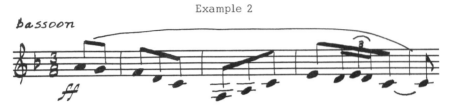

A brief motive (a very short musical subject — less than a melody) is played by the brass, then repeated by the woodwinds and strings:

Example 3

The bassoons introduce a lively theme:

Example 4

The next important theme is played alternately by the strings and woodwinds:

Example 5

Example 5 leads right into the next melody:

Example 6

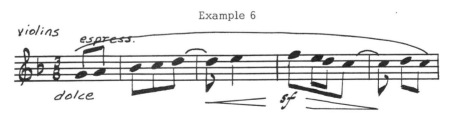

There is a brief transition which leads to Chabrier's original theme, Example 7. This melody is interrupted by parts of the malagueña theme, Example 1:

Example 7

trombones

The strings and woodwinds now play Example 1; this is followed by Example 2 played by the winds.

Repetitions of the motive of Example 3 lead to Example 5, now played by the bassoons and ornamented by the strings and flute. Example 5 is then repeated by the low strings with brass accompaniment.

Example 6 is played several times by various groups of instruments, leading to a loud dynamic climax.

Example 1 is played by the French horns; it is answered by the trombones.

A sequence (a motive or melody repeated on successive pitch levels) built on the trombone theme, Example 7, rises from the trombones and tuba, to the trumpets, finally to the woodwinds.

The rhapsody closes with fragments of the first theme, Example 1, played by various instruments, bringing the work to a rapid, rousing close.

> Meter: The regularly recurring accents or strong pulses in music, indicated by a time signature (2/4, 3/4, 4/4, 6/8, etc.). Those signatures in which the basic pulse involves two beats are called duple, while those with three are called triple. All other meters are compounded of combinations of these two.

> Rhapsody: Composers, starting in the late nineteenth-century, borrowed the expression "rhapsody" from poetry in which the term referred to an exciting or exaggerated legend or epic poem. Composers used the word to refer to instrumental compositions loosely constructed of several melodies which were treated in random fashion. Rhapsody often referred to music of a national character, such as Liszt's "Hungarian Rhapsodies" or Lalo's "Norwegian Rhapsody."

> Pizzicato: In Italian, pizzicato means "plucked." Composers use this expression for string passages in which

they wish the performer to sound a tone or tones by pluck-
ing the string with the finger rather than by sounding a
continuous tone by drawing the bow across the string.

Lyric : Another expression borrowed by the musician from
poetry is the adjective "lyric," by which the poet means
a verse of song-like nature or a stanza to be sung.
Hence, by this expression the composer means an instrumental melody meant to sound like a song.

Motive: A motive is the shortest melodic pattern that has
a memorable quality. It could be as short as two tones,
although most motives are one to two measures in length.

Sequence: By sequence, the musician means the repetition of the same melodic pattern at different pitch levels.

Emmanuel Chabrier

(January 18, 1841 – September 13, 1894)

Alexis Emmanuel Chabrier was born in Ambert, a city in south-cen-
tral France, about two-thirds of the way from Paris to Marseilles. For

him music was a hobby; he was
largely self-taught. It was not until he was in his thirties and resigned his job in the French Civil Service
that he decided to devote himself
entirely to his art.

Chabrier greatly admired the German operatic composer Richard Wagner; the Frenchman's own opera
"Gwendoline" (no longer performed)
is modeled on Wagner's still-popu-
lar opera "Tristan und Isolde." A-
nother composer who influenced
Chabrier and whom he befriended
was Cesar Franck.

Most of Chabrier's compositions
— several operas, a few orchestral
works, a quantity of piano pieces
and songs — were, for the most
part, conceived in a light vein. Today he is remembered principally by
his "España," which has been in the
repertory of most orchestras since
it was first introduced in 1883.

IN THE STEPPES OF CENTRAL ASIA

by Alexander Borodin

In the year 1880 a big celebration was organized in Russia to commemorate the twenty-fifth anniversary of the reign of Czar Alexander II. One of the highlights of this occasion was an exhibition of "living pictures" illustrating Russian history. For this celebration the Russian composer Alexander Borodin wrote one of his finest orchestral works, "In the Steppes of Central Asia."

Most Americans think of Russia as that country which borders central Europe on the east, yet Russia is a vast land stretching from the Baltic and Black Seas in Europe to the Pacific Ocean in Asia, from the Arctic Circle on the north to the Caspian Sea and Afghanistan in the south. In the province of Russia which borders on China, Kirghizia, there is a vast, treeless plain known as the steppes of Central Asia.

Borodin wrote a description of his new composition and had it printed in the conductor's score:

> "The silence of the sandy steppes of Central Asia is broken by the melody of a peaceful Russian song. The sad strains of Oriental tunes and the stamping of approach-

ing horses and camels are also heard. A caravan escorted by Russian soldiers crosses the unending desert and follows its way fearlessly, free from care, feeling safe in the protection of the Russian warriors. The caravan moves ever forward. The songs of the Russians blend with those of the natives of Asia, their tune gradually dying away in the distance."

The immensity and monotony of the vast desert plain are suggested by the long persistent violin tone — a high E — that begins at once and is sustained for fifty-three measures.

First a clarinet, then a horn play the "Russian theme" beneath the prolonged string tone:

Example 1

The peculiar, loping walk of camels is suggested by a rhythmic pattern played by low strings, pizzicato.

A melody of the Georgian territory — the "sad strain of an Oriental tune" — is played three times by the English horn:

Example 2

The pizzicato, rhythmic pattern is heard more clearly than before.

Example 1 returns, played in turn by the woodwinds, the brass, and then full orchestra. The increase in the dynamic level throughout this passage suggests the gradual approach of the Russian caravan. The pizzicato rhythm is played still more loudly.

The "Oriental theme" is heard three times in succession, the dynamic level becoming ever greater:

cellos and English horn
high strings
strings, an octave lower

The meeting of the two caravans is suggested as the two themes are combined four times (the top example in the following list in each case represents the higher pitched melody):

1) Example 1 - oboe
    Example 2 - violins

2) Example 1 - oboe
    Example 2 - cellos

3) Example 1 - flutes and violins
    Example 2 - bassoons and horns

4) Example 2 - flutes and violins
    Example 1 - English horn, violas and cellos

The first two measures of Example 1 are played, in turn, by:

French horns and clarinet
English horn and oboe
strings and oboe

As the pitch level becomes higher and higher, the dynamic level becomes quieter; the caravans disappear into the distance.

All of Example 1 is played by the clarinet. The high, sustained E in
the violins is heard again. Example 1 is repeated by the flute. The
music dies away.

> Pedal or Pedal Point: A sustained tone which persists
> through changes in harmony and melody in an extended
> passage is called a "pedal." The term comes from pipe
> organ music in which a sustained tone, usually in the
> bass or lowest part, is played by the foot pedal of the
> organ. (The high, sustained E for fifty-three measures in
> Borodin's "In the Steppes of Central Asia" is therefore
> called an "inverted pedal" since, instead of being in the
> bass, it is in the highest voice possible.)

> Counterpoint: The harmonious combination of two or more
> independent parts or melodies is called counterpoint. In
> sixteenth-century England, a melody was called a "point,"
> hence the expression "counterpoint" meaning "melody a-
> gainst melody." (The combination of Example 1 with Ex-
> ample 2 toward the end of "In the Steppes of Central
> Asia" is a fine example of this.)

Alexander Borodin

(November 12, 1833 - February 27, 1887)

Alexander Borodin was a member of "The Mighty Five," a group of
five Russian composers dedicated to the creation of music of a strongly

nationalistic flavor. Of the five — Balakirev, Cui, Mussorgsky, Rimsky-Korsakov, and Borodin — the last named was one of the most strongly nationalistic, using Russian and sometimes Oriental folk tunes, and, in programmatic music, relying heavily on folk stories and legends.

By training and profession, Borodin was a medical man and research chemist, writing several important books on such topics as aldehydes and fluorides. By nature , Borodin was a philanthropist, serving on the boards of numerous charitable organizations and actively working on welfare committees. For him music was a hobby, a pleasant pasttime. Unfortunately he had little leisure to spend with it.

The total number of compositions by Borodin is small, but most are important and worthy: an opera, "Prince Igor" (completed after his death by his friend Rimsky-Korsakov),

two symphonies (he was at work on a third when he died), two string quartets, a few fine songs, and the orchestral sketch, "In the Steppes of Central Asia."

ROMAN CARNIVAL OVERTURE

by Hector Berlioz

At the height of his creative period, French composer Hector Berlioz turned to an Italian subject for an opera: the career of Benvenuto Cellini, a sculptor and metalsmith of the sixteenth century (1500-1571). "I had been greatly struck with certain experiences in the life of Cellini" Berlioz wrote, "and was so unlucky as to think they offered an interesting and dramatic subject for an opera."

The opera failed at its first performance; it "was hissed with great energy by everyone! It was given three times at the opera house then disappeared from the stage."

From this unsuccessful opera Berlioz rescued the overture (prelude or instrumental work before the curtain opens) to the second act. He renamed it the "Roman Carnival Overture" since in the original opera the overture had included a lively tune used to accompany a fiery Italian dance — the saltarello — performed in Act II of the opera in a setting depicting one of the large squares in Rome.

The "Overture" opens with a bright and energetic theme played by the violins:

Example 1

After twenty measures, the brilliant opening gives way to a gracious theme played by the English horn accompanied by strings pizzicato:

Example 2

The violas repeat Example 2.

The cellos play Example 2 and are imitated one beat later by the flute,

oboe and violins playing the same melody in a higher octave. (This contrapuntal device is known as a <u>canon</u>.)

   Suddenly sweeping scale-like passages in quick succession are heard in the upper woodwinds:

Example 3

The saltarello or dance theme is introduced by the muted violins:

Example 4

(Note: The name "saltarello" comes from the Italian verb "saltare" meaning "to jump." A saltarello is usually in 6/8 meter with a jumping effect in its rhythm.)

   The saltarello theme is passed back and forth between the strings and woodwinds. The rhythm is reinforced by the cymbals, drums and triangle.

   Strings and woodwinds take up the sweeping runs of Example 3, interrupted intermittently by crashing chords for full orchestra.

   The dynamic level diminishes; the melody of Example 1 returns in a fugato passage (a fugato being a passage in contrapuntal form in which a melody is imitated in succession at differing pitch levels.)

   A crescendo (gradual increase in volume) leads back to the saltarello theme, Example 4, which is heard again in canonic imitation.

   As the "Overture" draws to a close the pace seems ever more frantic; the lyrical melody of Example 2 returns, now in counterpoint to the rhythm of the saltarello theme, Example 4.

   The "Overture" ends in a brilliant flash of orchestral color.

   <u>Overture</u> : An overture is an instrumental composition; originally the term was used to identify the introductory composition played before the opening of the curtain for an opera or stage play. Since the nineteenth century the expression has also been used to identify a single movement orchestral work which stands independent of any stage work; in this case it is sometimes called a <u>concert overture</u>.

Canon : A contrapuntal composition or passage in which one melodic part is imitated by one or more other parts, entering in such a way that the statements of the theme or melody overlap, is called a canon. Each statement is usually on the same pitch level, and if the melody leads back to a repetition of itself, the canon is endless as in the round "Three Blind Mice."

Fugato : A section of a composition is called a fugato if it is treated fugally even though the whole is not a fugue. This treatment consists of two or more contrapuntal voices (parts) which imitate each other, usually at the interval of the fifth and usually in succession (not overlapping entrances as in a canon).

Crescendo: In Italian the word crescendo means "increasing," hence in music it is used to indicate a passage in which the dynamics become louder. On the page of music it is usually indicated by the abbreviation cresc. or the symbol ◁. The opposite is diminuendo.

Hector Berlioz

(December 11, 1803-March 8, 1869)

The fondest hope of the elder Berlioz was that his son Hector should follow in his footsteps and become a doctor. To this end the boy took his first course in medicine when he was sixteen, and was enrolled in the Paris Medical School by his father when he was just eighteen. The school, in general, and the dissection room in particular, were too much for Hector Berlioz.

Against the pleadings of his father — and with the loss of his allowance — he quit. "I am convinced that I shall distinguish myself in music," he wrote back home, and added, "within me the voice of Nature is stronger than reason."

Although Berlioz composed a great many works, he is remembered chiefly for an important book he wrote on "Instrumentation" and for his compositions "Harold in Italy," for viola and orchestra, a dramatic symphony called "Romeo and Juliet," his Christmas work for chorus and orchestra called "The Childhood of Christ," his opera "The Trojans," and his youthful "Fantastic Symphony."

Chapter IV

THE REALM OF MUSIC

Music is an exciting language! As we have discovered through the music listening experiences outlined in earlier chapters of this book, a composer can take the constituent elements of music — rhythm, melody, harmony or counterpoint, timbre, dynamics and form — and create a wide variety of compositions. In this chapter we shall discover just such a variety. First we'll visit Paris with an American composer, then learn about a Spanish boy and his donkey through the music of an Italian-American composer, and finally we'll hear a bit of courtly Polish music written by a Polish composer who spent most of his life in Paris.

Through the listening ideas which you have discovered in this book, a "method" of listening to a new work for its melody and rhythm and form, you should be able to explore the entire realm of music. It is a wide, wide realm, for it includes jazz and rock and symphonic music. It includes music performed by ancient instruments, by modern synthesizers, by the human voice. It includes happy music and sad music. It includes music to think by, to dance to, and to sing with.

Now that you've started to explore the realm of music, don't stop. Enjoy this exciting world!

AN AMERICAN IN PARIS

by George Gershwin

When the American composer George Gershwin went to Paris in 1928, it was to learn what was going on in the French capital in the way of music. He wanted to hear the works of the "moderns" who were then at work in that city of lights: Darius Milhaud, Maurice Ravel, Igor Stravinsky, Serge Prokofiev, and Francis Poulenc. In between his sightseeing and his meetings with these composers, George Gershwin worked in his room at the Hotel Majestic on the sketches for "An American in Paris," playing bits of it over on the piano for such visitors to his room as Sir William Walton, the British composer laureate, and conductor Leopold Stokowski. Gershwin said of his new orchestral work:

33

"This new piece, really a rhapsodic ballet, is written freely and is the most modern music I've yet attempted. The opening part will be developed in typical French style, in the manner of Debussy and the Six, though the themes are all original. My purpose here is to portray the impression of an American visitor in Paris, as he strolls about the city, and listens to the various street noises and absorbs the French atmosphere.

"As in my other orchestral compositions I've not endeavored to represent any definite scenes in the music. The rhapsody is programmatic only in a general impressionistic way, so that the individual listener can read into the music such as his imagination pictures for him."[1]

In spite of the composer's remarks in the last paragraph, the following detailed program was printed for the premiere performance of the composition, and Gershwin allowed it to be printed in the published score, thus indirectly authorizing it. So if your "imagination" isn't great enough to "read into the music such as it pictures for you," you can perhaps follow this program as you listen to the music.

"You are to imagine an American, visiting Paris, swinging down the Champs-Élysées on a mild, sunny morning in May or June. Being what he is, he starts with preliminaries, and is off at full speed at once, to the tune of The First Walking Theme, a straightforward, diatonic air, designed to convey an impression of Gallic freedom and gaiety.

"Our American's ears being open, as well as his eyes, he notes with pleasure the sounds of the city. French taxi cabs seem to amuse him particularly, a fact that the orchestra points out in a brief episode introducing four Parisian taxi horns. These have a special theme alloted to them which is announced by the strings whenever they appear in the score.

"Having safely eluded the taxis, our American apparently passes the open door of a café, where, if one is to believe the trombones, "La Sorella" is still popular. Exhilerated by this reminder of the gay 1900s, he resumes his stroll through the medium of The Second Walking Theme, which is announced by the clarinet in French with a strong American accent.

"Both themes are now discussed at some length by the instruments, until our tourist happens to pass something. The composer thought it might be a church, while the commentator held out for the Grand Palais — where the Salon holds forth. At all events, our hero does not go in. Instead, as revealed by the English horn, he respectfully slackens his pace until he is safely past.

"At this point, the American's itinerary becomes somewhat obscured. It may be that he continues down the Champs-Élysées; it may be that he has turned off — the composer retains an open mind on the subject. However, since what immediately ensues is technically known as a bridge passage, one is reasonably justified in assuming that the Gershwin pen,

[1] George Gershwin, "An American in Paris," Musical America Dec. 1928

guided by an unseen hand, has perpetrated a musical pun, and that when The Third Walking Theme makes its eventual appearance, our American has crossed the Seine, and is somewhere on the Left Bank. Certainly it is distinctly less Gallic than its predecessors, speaking American with a French intonation, as befits that region of the city where so many Americans foregather. 'Walking' may be a misnomer, for despite its vitality, the theme is slightly sedentary in character, and becomes progressively more so. Indeed, the end of this section of the work is couched in terms so unmistakably, albeit pleasantly, blurred, as to suggest that the American is on the terrasse of a café, exploring the mysteries of an Anise de Lozo.

"And now the orchestra introduces the unhallowed episode. Suffice it to say that a solo violin approaches our hero (in soprano register) and addresses him in the most charming broken English; and, his response being inaudible — or at least unintelligible — repeats the remark. The one-sided conversation continues for some little time.

"Of course, one hastens to add, it is possible that a grave injustice is being done to both author and protagonist, and that the whole episode is simply a musical transition. The latter interpretation may well be true, for otherwise it is difficult to believe what ensues: our hero becomes homesick! He has the blues; and if the behavior of the orchestra be any criterion, he has them thoroughly. He realizes suddenly, overwhelmingly that he does not belong to this place, that he is the most wretched creature in all the world, a foreigner. The cool, blue Paris sky, the distant upward sweep of the Eiffel Tower, the bookstalls on the quay, the pattern of horse chestnut leaves on the white, sun-flecked street — what avails all this alien beauty? He is no Baudelaire, longing to be 'anywhere out of the world.' The world is just what he longs for, the world that he knows best; a world less lovely — sentimental and a little vulgar perhaps — but for all that, home.

"However, nostalgia is not a fatal disease — nor, in this instance, of overlong duration. Just in the nick of time the compassionate orchestra rushes another theme to the rescue, two trumpets performing the ceremony of introduction. It is apparent that our hero must have met a compatriot; for this last theme is a noisy, cheerful, self-confident Charleston, without a drop of Gallic blood in his veins.

"For the moment, Paris is no more; and a voluble, gusty, wise-cracking orchestra proceeds to demonstrate at some length that it's always fair weather when two Americans get together, no matter where. Walking Theme number two enters soon thereafter, enthusiastically abetted by number three. Paris isn't such a bad place, after all; as a matter of fact, it's a grand place! Nice weather, nothing to do until tomorrow. The blues return, but mitigated by the Second Walking Theme — a happy reminiscence rather than a homesick yearning — and the orchestra, in a riotous finale, decided to make a night of it. It will be great to get home; but meanwhile, this is Paris!"

George Gershwin

(September 28, 1898–July 11, 1937)

George Gershwin was born in Brooklyn, New York, in 1898. His name was recorded on his birth certificate as Jacob Gershvin. His father was an immigrant from Russia whose original name was Gershovitz.

George Gershwin's extraordinary career began when he was sixteen, playing the piano in music stores to demonstrate newly published popular songs of the day. His own popular song, "Swanee," written when he was nineteen, became immensely popular with more than a million copies of the music being sold, and more than two and a half million phonograph records of it.

There followed a series of highly successful Broadway shows, including "Lady Be Good" in 1924, "Strike Up the Band" in 1927, "Girl Crazy" in 1930, and "Of Thee I

Sing" in 1931 — a political satire which was the first musical to win a Pulitzer Prize.

The most important point in Gershwin's career was the creation of his "Rhapsody in Blue" for piano and symphony orchestra in which he applied the jazz idiom to an essentially classical form. This was followed by several successful works which combined the jazz idiom with more traditional forms: a "Concerto in F" (1925) for piano and orchestra; "An American in Paris (1928), a rhapsodic ballet; a "Cuban Overture" (1934); "Three Preludes for Piano" (1936); and his highly successful "Porgy and Bess" (1935), an American Negro folk opera.

Gershwin's death at the age of 38 from a brain tumor was a great loss to American art, for Gershwin has been the most significant composer America has produced to date.

PLATERO Y YO

by Mario Castelnuovo-Tedesco

During the Renaissance and the centuries that followed, the guitar was a very popular instrument. Then, during the nineteenth century, it fell out of favor except in Spain where it was still an important instrument for accompanying folk songs and dances. The guitar returned as a solo instrument of importance during the twentieth century largely through the artistic efforts of one man, Andrés Segovia, an extremely gifted guitar virtuoso.

At first Segovia programmed ancient classical guitar music on his recitals. He then started transcribing some of the keyboard music of Johann Sebastian Bach and his contemporaries. Finally, as the demand for guitar concerts grew, Segovia started asking outstanding twentieth-century composers to write new music for this ancient instrument.

The guitar music written by Mario Castelnuovo-Tedesco has been the finest to emerge from these requests of Segovia. Castelnuovo-Tedesco, who had written prize-winning operas, beautiful art songs and fine piano music, had never written for the guitar before. He invited Segovia to his home one evening and inquired about the range of the instrument, the technicalities of performance, and other questions to give the composer a better idea of how to write for the instrument. After an hour of conversation Castelnuovo-Tedesco had the answers to his questions. He started writing for the instrument the very next day. Segovia's comments about Castelnuovo-Tedesco's first guitar piece, "Variations As One Travels Through the Centuries" written in 1932, were significant. He said that the music sounded as though Castelnuovo-Tedesco had always known how to write for the instrument, had known its characteristics, its strengths, and was able to write superbly and idiomatically for the guitar.

In 1960 Mario Castelnuovo-Tedesco wrote a suite of twenty-eight

38

pieces (four sets of seven) for the guitar based on and inspired by a Spanish poem by Juan Ramón Jimenez which won the Nobel Prize in 1956. The poem was a simple story of a boy and his donkey. About the suite the composer has written:

> "My music for 'Platero and I,' from the poems for which Juan Ramón Jimenez won the Nobel Prize in 1956, was originally conceived as a set of twenty-eight pieces for narrator and guitar. ... Since most of the pieces are musically complete in themselves, they can be played in concert without a narrator. The poems deal with Platero, a small silver-gray donkey who accompanied the poet on his travels and was the confidant of his most intimate thoughts."

Platero (No. 1)

In this opening piece, the poet introduces the little trotting donkey. The poem, translated into English says:

> Platero is a small donkey,
> A soft, hairy donkey;
> So soft to the touch
> That it might be said
> To be made of cotton without bones.
>
> Only the black mirrors of his eyes
> Are hard like two black crystal scarabs.
> I turn him loose,
> And he goes to the meadow,
> And, with his nose,
> He gently caresses the little flowers
> Of rose and black and gold.

The piece opens with a guitar-like figure which suggests the trotting rhythm of Platero:

Example 1*

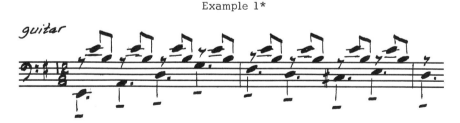

Melancolia (No. 7)

"Melancolia," which ends the first group of seven pieces, is a "tender elegy on the death of Platero," according to the composer. The poet, followed by a group of children, goes to visit the grave of Platero, while a white butterfly flutters in the air — perhaps it is the soul of the dead donkey."

Out of a repeated, descending arpeggio, an ecstatic melody arises, sad but beautiful:

Example 2

La Arrulladora (No. 18)

"La Arrulladora" means "The Lullaby." The poem tells us that in the forest the daughter of a poor charcoal-burner sings a lullaby to her little brother. The wind murmurs among the trees. The little child falls asleep, and Platero, too.

A song-like melody in the guitar opens the lullaby:

Example 3

Golondrinas (No. 23)

"Golondrinas" are swallows. In the spring, at the usual date, the swallows always come back. They chatter about their travels across the sea and the warm lands. But it is still cold here. Are the poor swallows going to freeze?

A fluttery, bird-like series of arpeggios for the guitar open this movement:

Example 4

Mario Castelnuovo-Tedesco

(April 3, 1895 - March 16, 1968)

Mario Castelnuovo-Tedesco was born in Florence, Italy. He began the study of music with his mother at the age of nine. She taught him to play the piano secretly because his rather stern father did not want a musician in the family. At the end of a year, however, when he played for his father two Chopin pieces and a composition of his own, resistance melted.

Then came intensive study, leading to a degree in piano at the age of fifteen, and a degree in composition at the age of eighteen. When he was nineteen, the great piano virtuoso Casella overheard him playing some Debussy. His teacher, Pizetti, told Casella he would find the young man's own compositions worth hearing. Casella listened, and immediately added them to his repertory.

In 1925 Castelnuovo-Tedesco's first opera, "La Mandragola" (The

Mandrake) based on Machiavelli's comedy, won the Italian Prize and was given its first performance in Venice in 1926. His opera, "Savonarola" was premiered in 1935 in the piazza in front of the old town hall of Medieval Florence, the setting of this story about the legendary Savonarola. An opera meant to be acted by puppets based on the Medieval story of "Aucassin and Nicolette" followed in 1938. His major opera, "The Merchant of Venice," won the International La Scala Prize in 1958.

The composer's major concertos have all been premiered by artists of international fame: his "Violin Concerto No. 2" by Jascha Heifetz and Arturo Toscanini in 1931; his "Concerto for Cello and Orchestra" by Gregor Piatigorsky and Toscanini in 1933; and both his guitar concertos by Andrés Segovia.

Castelnuovo-Tedesco left Italy in 1939 with his wife and two sons to escape anti-Semitism. (The family are Sephardic Jews whose home had originally been New Castile — "Castelnuovo" — in Spain.) Arturo Toscanini and Jascha Heifetz helped arrange Castelnuovo-Tedesco's admission into the United States where he eventually became a citizen. For a time the composer worked at MGM studios in Hollywood writing movie scores for such films as "The Loves of Carmen" starring Rita Hayworth. Asked by a reporter if coming to America had affected his symphonic style of writing, the composer replied: "Perhaps so, although I suppose one has to be born here to be really influenced by it. I love folk music; jazz is not my idiom. But, I love Gershwin! I think he is the greatest talent America ever had."

The works of William Shakespeare have inspired many of Castelnuovo-Tedesco's compositions including, of course, his opera "The Merchant of Venice." (Castelnuovo-Tedesco told this author that he learned English as a boy in Italy by reading Shakespeare and the King James version of the Bible.) Castelnuovo-Tedesco has written a series of Shakespeare songs based on the song-lyrics from the plays. He has set for voice a large number of the Shakespeare sonnets. The composer has also written a number of concert overtures to the Shakespeare plays, most of which were premiered by either Toscanini and the NBC Symphony, or Sir John Barbirolli and either the Vienna Philharmonic or the New York Philharmonic.

Mario Castelnuovo-Tedesco used the Bible as his other source of inspiration. He has written dramatic oratorios entitled: "The Book of Ruth" (for women's voices), "The Book of Jonah" (for men's voices), "The Song of Songs" (for mixed voices), and "Tobias and the Angels" (for student voices").

POLONAISE   IN   A - FLAT

Frédéric Chopin

Frédéric Chopin's first composition at the age of eight was a polonaise; at twelve, and again at sixteen, he composed polonaises. Yet this form took time for the composer to master; it did not leap from his pen in inspiration and complete mastery.

The polonaise is a slow dance, the rhythmic structure in triple meter being:

By origins, it was a dance of the nobility, a procession in grave and majestic style as of princes before their king. In its popular form, the polonaise retains the character of a dance that one walks to, or, better, glides to.

The A-flat major "Polonaise" (Opus 53) opens with an introduction based on a series of chords which move quickly up the chromatic scale:

Example 1

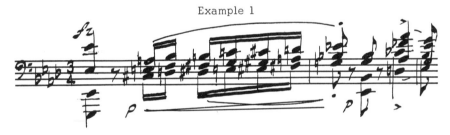

The main theme is heard immediately after the introduction, accompanied by octaves in the left hand:

Example 2

After the melody of Example 2 is finished, it is repeated more forcefully in octaves.

A new section is built on a figure which keeps moving within the initial octave span:

Example 3

A more lyrical theme is introduced:

Example 4

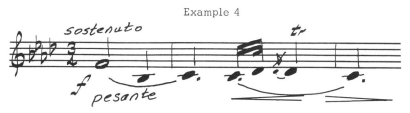

Example 4 is played in octaves and decorated with trills and runs, and leads immediately to a return of the melody of Example 2 in octaves, fortissimo.

A new section is introduced. The accompaniment pattern is heard first; after a series of rolled E-major chords, the left hand takes up a pattern of four descending notes in octaves. The melody appears over this continuously repeated bass pattern:

Example 5

The music changes key briefly, then returns to the original tonality as Example 5 is heard again. Once again the music changes key, this time more boldly. As the force of the passage subsides, a new, lighter theme is introduced in D major:

Example 6

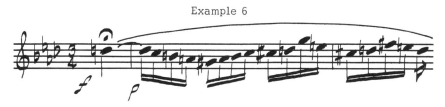

After Example 6 has been expanded and developed, a crescendo leads to a return of the melody of Example 2 in octaves, fortissimo.

A powerful, five-octave scale moves upward across the keyboard, leading to the final statement of the melody of Example 2 in the upper octaves of the piano. A series of chords concludes the polonaise.

Frédéric François Chopin

(March 1, 1810 - October 17, 1849)

Frédéric Chopin was born in Zelazowa Wola, Poland, of a French father and a Polish mother. His father had moved to Poland as a young man and served for a time as a bookkeeper in a tobacco firm run by a Frenchman. After losing that position, he took a job as tutor in one of the wealthier Polish homes. He fell in love with the housekeeper of the estate, a Polish girl, and they were married. Frédéric was the second child of this marriage.

Frédéric started piano lessons at the age of six; two years later the boy tried his hand at composition for the first time. He was later enrolled at the high school in Warsaw where he studied music among other subjects. Although Chopin received no private piano lessons after his twelfth year, he continued to practice the piano as well as work on original compositions. When he was fifteen, he was presented with a diamond ring by the Czar for his pianistic ability. In the same year he prepared his first manuscript for publication, "Rondo in C Major."

When Chopin was nineteen, he went with three of his friends for a visit to Vienna, Munich and Paris. Shortly after that Chopin moved to Paris where he lived the rest of his life. Of frail health, Chopin spent his adult life playing in the fashionable salons of Paris and writing a series of brilliant works for piano in the small forms then popular: preludes, etudes (or studies), polonaises, mazurkas (another Polish dance form), waltzes, ballades, impromptus and nocturnes.

Chapter V
MUSIC AND DANCE

Life is extremely rhythmical. We live, breath, walk, run, play and talk with rhythmic movement. The entire universe around us moves rhythmically. Perhaps this explains why rhythm is the element in music which sometimes appeals to us first, which we understand most easily.

We become aware of rhythm as a pattern of duration, stress, release and pause, organized for an expressive purpose.

Rhythm is essential in music, but it can exist independently of music. The rhythm of music is created by the relative duration of its tones and periods of silence. Since tone is the basic characteristic of music, we better understand rhythm when we associate it with a tonal pattern (a motive or melody).

As an example, sing through the melody from the opening of this well-known American song, "The Battle Hymn of the Republic":

Mine eyes have seen the glory of the coming of the Lord

You will discover that a rhythm pattern, ♪ ♩ , is repeated throughout, a pattern involving a tone of short duration followed by one three times longer. Notice also, as you sing this melody, that the first tone in each measure has more of a stress than any other tone in it; the tone at the mid-point of each measure (the third "beat" or pulse) receives the next strongest stress known as a secondary accent.

Try singing the melody to discover if there are any points of release or pause. Sing through the entire song to find recurrences of the basic rhythm pattern; look also for the places in the song where the most obvious pauses occur.

In the music in this chapter, all of which is dance music, the composers have relied principally on the element of rhythm to suggest the nature of each work. Try to discover, as you listen to these compositions, how these dances differ, largely as a result of various types of rhythms employed.

45

RUMANIAN FOLK DANCES

by Béla Bartók

Rumania is a very old country on the Black Sea in southeast Europe. When the Hungarian composer Béla Bartók visited this neighboring country of Rumania in 1909, he became fascinated with the folk tunes that he heard while traveling around. He immediately made up his mind that he would return so that he could jot down some of these wonderful melodies.

For four years Bartók roamed around Rumania, visitng small villages and hamlets, going wherever he thought he could find peasants who knew the ancient folk dances and melodies. Some of the tunes that he heard he wrote down in musical notation; others he recorded on a crude, hand-wound phonograph.

In 1915 Bartók took seven of the dance tunes that he had collected and made them into a dance suite (a group of contrasting, separate movements) for piano. When completed, his "Rumanian Folk Dances" were so popular everywhere, friends encouraged him to score (instrument) the suite for small orchestra.

Joc cu bâtă

One evening at a small village tavern Bartók heard a gypsy violinist play a beautiful old folk tune, "Joc cu bâtă." It was a melody from the Maros-Torda district of Transylvania, one used to accompany a dance - game played with sticks. ("Joc cu bâtă" means "dance with sticks.") The gaily syncopated melody was both merry and energetic.

The composer made very few changes in the tune when he used it in the first movement of his dance suite. To keep the original character of the music, he assigned the melody to the orchestral violins. Simple chords accompany it.

Such chords serve as an introduction to the dance, establishing immediately the basic pulse: duple meter, or, in musical notation, a grouping by bar lines of two beats per measure, a strong (accented one) followed by one of lesser stress.

In the fourth measure, the clarinet and first violins play the gypsy melody, Example 1, while the rhythm of the dance is provided by the harmony of the second violins, violas, cellos and bass viols.

* Copyright 1918 by Universal Edition; Renewed 1945. Copyright and renewal assigned to Boosey & Hawkes, Inc., for the U.S.A. Reprinted by permission.

Example 1, with its rhythm varied slightly, is repeated.
The violins play Example 2, a melody which ends pizzicato.

Example 2

With very slight changes, Example 2 is repeated. This brings this short dance movement in binary form to a close.

>Binary Form: If we do as we did before, assign letters of the alphabet to each theme, we need two letters, a and b. The dance then could be outlined: a - a - b - b, or, essentially an A and a B section. The musician calls this two-part or binary form, a very popular structure for dances.

>Rhythm Patterns: In addition to the basic pulse of this dance, notice the composer's repeated use of memorable rhythm groups, Figures A and B. These are called rhythm patterns or rhythmic motives.

Pe loc

The third dance of the suite is based on a melody that Bartók heard Rumanian peasants playing on a primitive, hand-made flute of wood. The tune was used to accompany a stamping dance which was performed in one spot. ("Pe loc" means "on the spot.") The dance is a slow one with a steady step; the melody, almost like a bagpipe tune, is constructed of small intervals (the distance between two tones).

"Pe loc" is also in duple meter, but a much slower dance than "Joc cu bătă." Once again the rhythm is established by introductory chords, and, Bartók has preserved the original flavor of this dance by assigning the melody to the piccolo (a very small flute, correctly a "piccolo flauto" or "tiny flute").

Example 3

The piccolo continues, playing a melody twice as long as the first. It begins:

Example 4

The first nine measures of this theme, Example 4, are repeated. A brief closing section of four measures brings the dance to its conclusion.

Notice that in this dance, both melodies — Examples 3 and 4 — employ syncopation. (Described on page 17 in detail.) Notice too that this dance is in binary form, but in this case the first melody, Example 3, is not repeated.

Béla Bartók

(March 25, 1881 - September 26, 1945)

Béla Bartók was born in a little Hungarian village where his father was the Director of the School of Agriculture and his mother was a teacher. When Béla was eight, his father passed away. His mother then had to rear her family on a very meagre income.

In spite of great poverty, the mother managed to work and to teach her son the piano. Béla composed his first musical work when he was

nine; a year later he made his piano debut.

The composer became interested in Hungarian folk songs when he was studying at the Liszt Academy in Budapest and spent many years collecting more than six thousand folk tunes. Much of his music reflects this folk song influence.

When the Nazi Germans started capturing most of southeastern Europe in the late 1930s, Bartók fled to New York City where he became a professor of music at Columbia University. His years in this country were not happy ones. His income was very small, he missed his beloved homeland, and he was in very bad health.

He is remembered chiefly for his "Concerto for Orchestra," three piano concertos, "Mikrokosmos" (a series of graded pieces for the piano), "Music for Strings, Percussion and Celeste" and his folk song suites.

THE AGE OF GOLD

by Dmitri Shostakovich

The government of Soviet Russia has tried many times since the 1917 Revolution to encourage — even command — its artists (writers, painters and composers) to create works that represent the political philosophy of Communism. One of Russia's most famous and talented composers, Dmitri Shostakovich, has followed this path; his ballet, "The Age of Gold," is an example.

The ballet was written in 1931. It is a spoof of western society, which, in the eyes of the Russians, is governed by the value and importance of gold. The story concerns the adventures of a Soviet football team in a foreign city during a World's Fair. Music-hall scenes alternate with scenes on the sports ground, the players being tempted away from the championship game with all the mystery of a detective novel.

Polka

The "Polka" occurs in one of the music-hall scenes which bears the sub-title, "Once Upon a Time in Geneva." Actually the story is not the only comic element, for the music itself is a spoof of the polka.

The introduction is brief and humorous. An E-flat clarinet (smaller and higher pitched than the regular clarinet) plays a brief, awkward ascending (rising) pattern against a bassoon accompaniment. The French horns respond with repeated, harsh-sounding chords. The strings (pizzicato) then establish the basic pulse of the dance.

The xylophone introduces the principal melody, an awkward one filled with wide leaps:

Example 1*

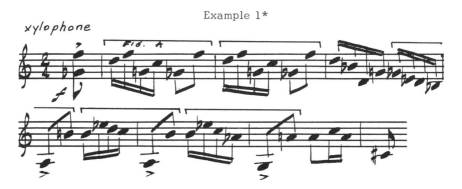

Two measures later the saxophone responds with another melody, one which is completed by the E-flat clarinet:

Example 2

The trumpet continues in a passage in which the melody is a rhythmic variant of Example 2.

Still a third saucy tune is introduced:

Example 3

Accompanied by triangle and wood block, the upper woodwinds play a series of rhythmical but dissonant (non-harmonious) chords. The woodwinds repeat this passage.

The strings respond with a variant of Example 1; the woodwinds answer with a pert little melodic fragment. The trombone is heard, then the woodwinds again.

A solo bassoon, unaccompanied, plays a figure that rises from its lowest tones.

The xylophone repeats the principal theme, Example 1. The trumpet responds with Example 3, whose final measure is changed in order to lead to the few sharp chords that end the "Polka."

> Polka: A polka is a lively dance in duple meter which originated in Bohemia around 1830. One of its chief rhythmical characteristics is the strong stress at the mid-point of each measure; a pause or lift sometimes occurs just before the first pulse of a measure.

Dmitri Shostakovich

(September 25, 1906 –   )

Dmitri Shostakovich had the good fortune to become famous overnight. It occurred on May 12, 1926, when the Leningrad Philharmonic gave the first performance of this nineteen-year-old's "Symphony No. 1." The composition had been his final project as a student at the Conservatory.

The composer's parents had moved from their native Siberia to St. Petersburg when Dmitri was born in 1906. Both parents were musical: his father as an amateur singer, his mother as a music teacher. Shostakovich wrote of his youth: "In our apartment we held amateur musical evenings. This impressed itself on my musical memory and played a certain part in my future work as a composer. "

His early works alternate between the politically oriented works such as his "Symphony No. 2" dedicated to the October Revolution of 1917 and the "Symphony No. 3" (The "May Day" Symphony) and the satirical as suggested in his opera, "The Nose" and the ballet, "The Age of

Gold."

Over the years he has been both looked upon with favor by the government and called to task for writing music that was "thoroughly non-political." He is best known for his fifteen symphonies, the opera "Lady Macbeth of Mtzensk" (now known as "Katerina Izmailova"), a piano concerto and numerous short works for piano.

THE BARTERED BRIDE

by Bedřich Smetana

The opera, "The Bartered Bride," is a comedy; its locale is a small village somewhere in Bohemia (now Czechoslovakia). The story is quite a complicated one, involving a case of mistaken identity. Jenik is in love with Marenka, whose parents, however, want her to marry the stupid, stammering Vasek (son of the wealthy Micha). He agrees with the marriage-broker to give up Marenka in return for a payment of money on the condition that Marenka shall marry Micha's son. As Jenik turns out to be a son of Micha by an earlier marriage, he gets the best of the bargain — both the money and the bride.

The first act of the opera ends with the young people of the village dancing in the square outside the village inn. They dance the famous Bohemian polka, a lively, skipping dance in duple meter. The dance takes its name from the fact that there is a strong pulse half-way through each measure (the second beat); "polka" is the Bohemian word for "half."

Later, in the village inn, all the young people dance the furiant, a rapid and fiery dance. Syncopation, or the use of misplaced accents, is one of its chief characteristics. The name "furiant" is derived from the adjective "furiously," suggesting that the dance is performed as fast as possible.

Polka

During the introduction to the dance, in which the strings, timpani and horns are prominent, there is a general flurry on stage as the older people find seats under the trees in order to watch the young dancers.

The first of several tunes is introduced by the clarinets and violins:

Example 1

Following several repetitions of Example 1, the strings introduce a quieter theme:

Example 2

The theme of Example 2 then becomes the accompaniment to Example 3:

Example 3

The strings play a new melody, Example 4, which is lighter in nature, softer and more staccato. It is based on the rhythm pattern of Example 2.

Example 4

The opening melody, Example 1, returns, now livelier than ever. In the original version for stage performance, the villagers join the music, singing:

> Join our dancing, swaying, dancing
> While the tuneful polka's playing;
> Cheek to cheek with hand in hand
> Twirling to the village band!
>
> Basses growling, cymbals clinking,
> 'Round our ears the music's tinkling.
> Though for quiet we may strive
> 'Neath our feet the earth's alive.

Furiant

A brief introduction summons the dancers:

Example 5

The principal theme of the dance (from which the introductory Example 5 was derived) is announced by the violins:

Example 6

There is a sudden contrast as the low strings and bassoon play a quiet, chromatic theme (moving by half-steps) while the oboe takes up a graceful accompaniment:

Example 7

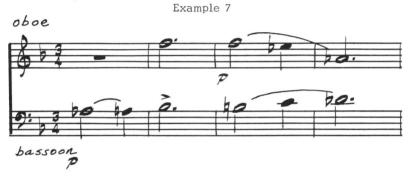

Soon the energetic atmosphere of the first section, based on Example 6, returns, leading this dance in ternary form to a boisterous ending.

> Furiant: A fast, fiery dance in triple meter, usually ternary form. One of its chief characteristics is its use of syncopation.

> Nationalism: An effort among nineteenth-century composers to make their music representative of their native land through the use of folk tunes, native rhythms, and, when the music was programmatic, the use of folk legends or stories. The movement originated in Russia and spread to Bohemia, Norway and Hungary.

Bedřich Smetana

(March 2, 1824 - May 12, 1884)

At age sixteen Bedřich Smetana started to keep a diary. In it he said of his childhood: "I was born in Bohemia, the son of a master brewer. I was not quite four when my father taught me how to keep time to music. At five I started to school and studied the piano and violin. I was seven when I first performed in public."

Although Smetana's parents disliked the idea of their son preparing for a career in music (they thought it fine for a hobby but not for earning money) he pursued music as his major interest throughout his school days.

He developed as a composer during troubled times for his native land. Long dominated by the Hungarians or the Germans, Bohemia revolted in 1848 for its independence. It was short-lived and Bohemia was then once again controlled by the Germans.

Much of the music for which Smetana is remembered reflects his strong nationalistic feelings; " Ma Vlast" ("My Country"), a tone poem for orchestra; "From My Life" for string quartet; and his opera "Dalibor" (Dalibor was a legendary hero involved in the liberation of Czechoslovakia) and "Libuse" (Libuse was the founder of the city of Prague, the Czech capital).

Chapter VI
MUSIC OF FAITH

In the earliest days of music a singer performed his music without any accompaniment — probably because even the crudest instruments had yet to be invented. Traces of this ancient practice may be found in the music performed in our present-day houses of worship. In some of the Jewish services, particularly during the High Holy Days, a Cantor might perform the chants and scriptural readings in unaccompanied song. Occasionally a Roman Catholic service will make use of ancient Gregorian chants in which several voices sing the same melodic line in unison, without accompaniment.

Today, however, we are more accustomed to hearing "something" accompanying the melodic line. It usually is a series of chords (three or more pitches sounded simultaneously):

It might be, however, as in the case of a round, the same melody being sung at different times by two, three, four or more groups of singers:

Rarely is an unaccompanied melody heard. The traditional bugle calls of the Army are some of the final remnants of this type:

When a melody is accompanied by chords — as in the case of "America" — the musical fabric or texture is said to be harmonic. When a melody is pitted against itself or another melody in a contrapuntal manner, the musical texture is said to be polyphonic ("polyphonic" meaning "many-voiced"). When a melody is unaccompanied, the texture is said to be monophonic ("single voiced").

Harmony is that element of music which pertains to chords. A chord, as mentioned earlier in this chapter, is a combination of three or more different pitches heard simultaneously. In its broadest meaning, harmony refers to chordal movement — the progression of one chord to another.

In contrapuntal or polyphonic music, each voice (whether a human voice or the voice of a violin, trumpet or other instrument) is independent, or, in common terms, all parts have a "melody." There can be rhythmic independence among the voices. On the other hand, all voice parts may move in essentially the same rhythm, yet the individual voices are created linearly (in a horizontal line as opposed to vertical chords).

In this chapter you will discover music that has been inspired and created by faith in a higher power, in God. Sometimes the composer has used a harmonic setting for his melodies; in other instances he has created music that is contrapuntal or polyphonic. Listen carefully so that you can learn to hear the difference in the musical fabric or texture.

JESUS CHRIST SUPERSTAR

by Andrew Lloyd Webber

A strange thing happened in music during the late 1960s. After several hundred years of being relegated to use in houses of worship, music based on religious subjects became part of everyday life! Albums such as "Jesus Christ Superstar" and "Godspell" headed the weekly sales charts. Young people flocked to record stores to buy copies. Disc jockeys regularly scheduled selections from the albums on their radio shows. "Jesus Christ Superstar" was such a hit album that its creators, the composer Andrew Lloyd Webber and the lyricist and author of the book Tim Rice , cast it into a fully staged Broadway musical, calling it a "rock opera." In London, New York and Tokyo it became an overnight success. Soon road-show companies were performing it all over the United States. In the fall of 1973 it was released as a movie, having been filmed "on location" in Israel!

Actually "Jesus Christ Superstar" was not the first venture of Andrew Lloyd Webber and Tim Rice into the field of sacred music. These two artists, both of them British, first met each other in 1965. Their first co-operative project was to try and write a musical based on the life of Dr. Bernardo. This failed to get off the ground. They then wrote a few pop

songs during the next two or three years, some of which were recorded, but none of which achieved any degree of success.

Finally, in 1968, they decided to write a "pop oratorio" for use in schools based on the Biblical story of Joseph and his coat of many colors. They called their work, "Joseph and His Amazing Technicolor Dreamcoat." Both in England and in the United States this "pop oratorio" was performed by countless school choirs, orchestras and pop groups. It was a success among the students for whom it was created, but the record album of it was not very successful. In fact, it wasn't even released in the United States until some three years after it was created, after "Jesus Christ Superstar" had become a hit album.

After "Joseph and His Amazing Technicolor Dreamcoat," Webber and Rice decided to use the Passion story, the Biblical account of the last seven days of Jesus of Nazareth on earth for a musical. Johann Sebastian Bach, among many others, had done the same thing several hundred years earlier. Bach used the story as told by Matthew in the first book of the New Testament as the basis for his oratorio, "The Passion According to St. Matthew." Later, the twentieth-century composer, Stephen Schwartz, was to use the same Biblical account of Matthew as the basis for his successful Broadway musical, "Godspell."

Tim Rice, who created the book and words for "Jesus Christ Superstar," decided to tell the story from a slightly different point of view than the traditional version of St. Matthew. Rice made Judas, the traitor, the protagonist or central character in the story of Jesus. Judas is portrayed as a close personal friend of Jesus, his "right-hand man." In fact, Judas is such a close friend that he cannot conceive that Jesus might be more than just another human, that he might be the Son of God. Throughout the early part of the show, Judas cautions Jesus, saying: "They think they've found the new Messiah, and they'll hurt you when they find they're wrong."

Because "Jesus Christ Superstar" is a rock opera, almost every musical selection is set to a rock beat. "Everything Is Alright" is a good example, for it is sung by Mary Magdalene to a slow rock beat. The meter is 5/4, five beats to the measure. (This used to be an unusual meter signature, but Bartok made it quite common in symphonic music of the twentieth century, and Dave Brubeck introduced it into popular music of the twentieth century with his "Take Five.")

Mary Magdalene is a sinner whom Jesus has forgiven. As evening of the first day approaches, Mary Magdalene tries to comfort Jesus, telling him to "sleep well tonight."

Example 1*

Try not to get wor-ried, try not to turn on to

Prob-lems that up - set you

"Everything Is Alright" is in ternary or three-part song form. Twice we hear the section that begins as in Example 1. An interlude or middle section follows based on a rising melodic figure. It is sung by Judas as he questions Mary Magdalene's use of "fine ointments — brand new and expensive" to wash the feet of Jesus.

The original melody of Example 1 returns as Mary Magdalene repeats the words of the opening stanza.

Andrew Lloyd Webber

(March 22, 1948 -   )

Born in London, Andrew Lloyd Webber comes from a very musical family. His father is a well-known composer and organist in England, and is now Director of the London College of Music. Andrew Lloyd Webber had his first composition published when he was but nine years of age! Later he won a Queen's Scholarship to the Westminster School, and then a

scholarship in history to Magdalen College, Oxford University. He left Oxford to study music at the Royal College of Music.

Mr. Lloyd Webber first met Tim Rice in 1965, and after writing some pop tunes, they cooperated in creating the pop oratorio already mentioned, "Joseph and His Amazing Technicolor Dreamcoat." Following the success of the stage version of "Jesus Christ Superstar," Mr. Lloyd Webber helped prepare the movie version of it, and composed the musical score for the movie, "Gumshoe."

PASSIO ET MORS DOMINI NOSTRI JESU CHRISTI

SECUNDUM LUCAM

by Krzysztof Penderecki

The contemporary Polish composer, Krzysztof Penderecki, has written many large works for chorus, orchestra and soloists. One of the finest recounts the Passion story, the account of the last seven days of Jesus of Nazareth on earth. Penderecki based his oratorio on the version of the story by St. Luke, and is called (in English) "The Passion and Death of Our Lord Jesus Christ According to St. Luke."

Penderecki's "Passion" was commissioned by the West German Radio to mark the 700th anniversary of the Münster Cathedral, and was begun in 1963 and completed in 1965. The first performance of it was in the cathedral itself.

Just before the first performance of his "St. Luke Passion," Penderecki told some reporters: "I am a Roman Catholic. In my opinion, however, one does not have to belong to a church to compose religious music. The only condition is that one is willing to confess one's religious convictions. Therefore, you can without any objection consider my music as avowal music; in that respect, I am a Romanticist."

The "St. Luke Passion" is scored for large orchestra, soprano, baritone and bass soloists, narrator (whose part is spoken), a children's choir, and three adult choruses. The work is in two parts, each of which is through-composed, that is, without any repeated sections or parts. Being a modern work, it is not really in any of our regular keys or tonalities, although much of it centers around the pitch of the note $\underline{D}$. In style the work includes some old-fashioned polyphonic passages, some chorus parts that are declaimed or spoken rather than sung, and a bit of chance or aleatoric writing in which passages are performed a different way each time the work is performed, leaving to chance the actual sound.

Following the tradition of Johann Sebastian Bach's "St. Matthew Passion" and "St. John Passion" of 275 years earlier, Penderecki's work tells the story of Jesus last seven days in the words of the Gospel according to St. Luke, with both personal and communal responses to the story. The soloists and the chorus all function as characters in the drama. The text, in Latin, is taken from the "Gospel According to St. Luke" as found in the New Testament. Penderecki's "Passion" starts with Chapter 22, Verse 39, and concludes with Chapter 23, Verse 36. He omits some thirty verses because of the time element in the performance of the music.

What makes Penderecki's "Passion" a completely individual work are the powerful and dramatic effects he achieves in his treatment of both instrumental and vocal sound. The conductor's score is full of most unusual directions to the players, telling them to do such things as to rub the back of the violin bow on a hard surface, and aleatoric or chance passages between high and low points in an instruments range. Many of the things he suggests are the result of his own experiments with the nature of sound.

His choirs make hissing and jeering sounds to suggest the rabble of the crowd as Jesus is brought before Pilate. Sometimes Penderecki even divides the syllables of a word between different voices in the choir, thus giving an almost three-dimensional effect of space and distance such as would be occupied by the babbling crowd. Yet, in their seemingly confused fragments, the words are still recognizable and can be understood.

Penderecki's methods, however, are not tricks or gimmickry for its own sake. He follows the tradition of the eighteenth-century German composer, Heinrich Schütz, who tried in his "St. Matthew Passion" to imitate the sound of the cock crowing during Peter's denial, and the many cases in the Passion music of Bach in which the composer attempted to make realistic suggestions of angels rising to heaven, and so on.

Some of the most interesting passages of Penderecki's work are in a style we call _aleatoric_ writing, passages in which "alea" or "chance" plays an important part. One such section is that based on the following:

Et surgens omnis multitudo eorum,	And the whole multitude of them, rising up,
Duxerunt illum ad Pilatum,	Led Him to Pilate,
Coeperunt autem accusare Dicentes:	And they began to accuse him, Saying:
"Hunc invenimus subvertentem gentem nostram,	"We have found this man perverting our nation,
Et prohibentem tributa dare Caesari,	And forbidding to give tribute to Caesar,
Et dicentem se Christum Regem esse."	And saying that he is Christ the King."

Starting with the Latin phrase "invenimus subvertentem," the composer assigns the syllables to different voices, and then allows every person to progress at his own rapid chance or aleatoric speed.

The phrase "Christum regem esse" is then shouted together. Choir I's portion of this, Example 1, will illustrate the point. The dramatic effect is that after the self-centered "we have found" (which occurs just before the music of Example 1), the crowd mutters to each other and then builds to a climax as they accuse Jesus of refusing to pay tribute to Caesar, and, even worse, claiming that He "himself is Christ the King."

Example 1

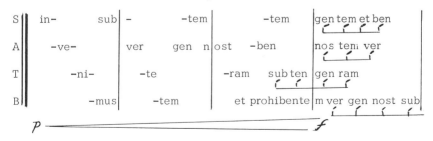

S	repeat word	phrase 3 times			Christum regem	es-se
A	repeat word	phrase 4 times		et dicentem se	Christum regem	es-se
T	repeat word	phrase twice	et prohibentem Caesari		Christum regem	es-se
B	repeat word	phrase twice			Christum regem	es-se

Oratorio: A setting of a text on a sacred or epic theme for chorus, soloists and orchestra, for performance in a church or concert hall.

Aleatoric Music: Music in which chance plays an important part. "Alea" literally means "dice," and thus aleatoric music leaves certain factors to chance just as throwing dice leaves their numeric outcome to chance.

Krzysztof Penderecki

(November 23, 1933 –   )

Krzysztof Penderecki was born in 1933 at Debica, Poland. He studied composition in Cracow and graduated from the Conservatory of Music with honors in 1958. Attention was first drawn to him in 1959 when he anonymously entered three different compositions in a competition sponsored by the Youth Circle of the Association of Polish Composers and won the first three prizes!

The following year Penderecki won third prize in the Polish Radio's contest. In 1961 his "Threnody 'To the Victims of Hiroshima'" was given a mark of recommendation and distinction by ENESCO's "Tribune Internationale des Compositeurs."

CANTATA NO. 147

by Johann Sebastian Bach

For most of the sixty-five years of his life, Johann Sebastian Bach was a devout church musician. He started to play the pipe organ for Sunday services when he was nine, and, with the exception of a few years spent in the employ of the Duke of Weimar, he regularly directed the choir, played the organ and composed sacred music for every Sabbath of his life. He said, "The aim and final reason of all music should be for the Glory of God."

Bach was a Lutheran. For their services he composed five sets of cantatas, each set containing a different cantata for every Sunday of the liturgical year, a total of 295 cantatas of which 202 have survived.

The cantata (from the Italian verb "cantare" meaning "to sing") usually consists of several movements which are linked together by the text, and may be based melodically on the same choral or hymn tune. The various movements are set as solos, duets and choruses. The instrumentation or accompaniment varies widely in the cantatas of Bach, for he usually scored the cantata for whatever instrumentalists he had at his disposal at the time.

Jesu, Joy of Man's Desiring

Chorals (sometimes spelled "chorales"), the congregational hymns, were a heritage of the Lutheran church, dating back to the earliest days of the Reformation. Frequently Bach borrowed a choral by another composer for the melodic basis of his cantatas. This is the case with his Cantata No. 147. The original was a choral called "Come Awake" by Johann Schop that Bach found in a hymnal printed in 1642. Bach immediately harmonized it:

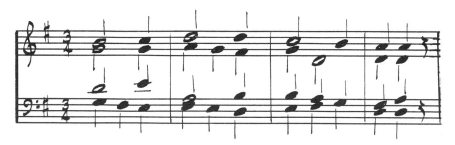

For the chorus of his Cantata No. 147, Bach broke up the choral lines with instrumental interludes (short sections which melodically contrast with the sections on either side of them). These interludes are all based on the flowing melody heard in the introduction:

Example 1

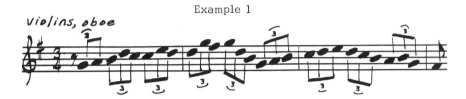

The choir enters with the first line of the text of the choral:

Example 2

Jesu, Joy of man's desiring
Holy Wisdom, Love most bright;

An interlude of six measures, derived from Example 1, is heard before the first melodic line of the choral is repeated, this time with a different text:

Drawn by Thee, our souls aspiring
Soar to uncreated light.

After the next orchestral interlude, the choir enters with a melody closely related to that of Example 2:

Word of God, our flesh that fashioned,
With the glow of faith impassioned.

A two-measure interlude leads to the return of the melody of Example 2, making the choral itself in ternary form. The text on the repetition is:

Striving still to Truth unknown,
Life attaining near Thy throne.

A ten-measure orchestral postlude, based on Example 1, ends the work.

Cantata: The Italian verb "cantare" means "to sing"; the Italian verb "sonare" means "to play." Originally the term cantata was used to designate any vocal composition while the word sonata was used to designate any instrumental composition. The group of works which are called cantatas include very diverse compositions, some sacred, some secular. Some are set for a single solo voice, but most make use of several soloists and choir. A few are scored for accompaniment by a single keyboard instrument; most are scored for an orchestra.

Choral or Chorale: The original hymn tunes of the Reformed or Lutheran church were called chorals. The first were published in 1524; these were adapted from hymns already in use in the Roman Catholic Church, from secular songs and some were original hymns. Most chorals are harmonized for four voices: soprano, alto, tenor and bass.

Interlude: The word has several uses in music, all of which refer to a contrasting phrase or section which occurs in the middle of a larger work. Frequently it is used to designate the instrumental phrase between the lines of a song or choral.

Johann Sebastian Bach

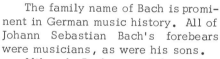

(March 21, 1685 – July 28, 1750)

The family name of Bach is prominent in German music history. All of Johann Sebastian Bach's forebears were musicians, as were his sons.

Although Bach served for a time as a court musician, writing instrumental works for the orchestra of the court, he spent most of his adult life as a church organist, choir director and composer in the Lutheran churches of northern Germany. For Sunday services he wrote more than 200 sacred cantatas, a setting of the Mass, and several settings of the Passion.

Although most of Bach's contemporaries moved widely throughout Europe, Bach never traveled farther than 250 miles from the town of his birth in his entire lifetime!

In addition to his sacred choral works, Bach is well known for his six "Brandenburg Concertos" for orchestra, and his "Well Tempered Clavier."

Chapter VII

MUSIC AND IMAGINATION

Music is an abstract language; it doesn't speak in specifics. It is also a language of fantasy.

The music of this chapter is music of fantasy, of imagination, of dreams. When one recalls a dream, it is seldom clearly defined. One remembers a hint of pleasure or sadness, a floating experience, the glimpse of a familiar place, but all clouded with the mist of unreality.

At the beginning of the twentieth century, a group of composers — led by Claude Debussy — was fascinated by this world of dreams. They became musical poets of nature, not as the eyes sees nature, but of nature as sensed. They didn't deal with scenes as a realistic painter would, but rather with the feelings suggested by the scenes. In their music they attempted to suggest rather than to describe accurately, to reflect not the object itself, but the emotional reaction to the object, to interpret a fleeting impression rather than to capture and fix the permanent reality. This they did through sound and light and color — a world of musical fantasy. They were musical poets "of mists and fountains, clouds and rain; of dusk and glints of sunlight through leaves."[1] They were "moonstruck and seastruck" and "lost soul(s) under a sky besprent with stars. ... There was touch as well as sight in these sensations, and in all a wealth of fantasy, as if (one) not only saw but heard the dancing of shadows on velvet feet."

The success of your listening to the music in this chapter does not depend on your knowledge or understanding of its form, its technical structure. Rather, the magic spell of its tonal beauty should capture your imagination; musical details should be forgotten and give way to the atmosphere the music creates. For it is through the composer's use of "musical color" — or "timbre" to use the technical word — that these fantasies are suggested by the composer and re-created in the listener's mind.

NOCTURNES

by Claude Debussy

In the year 1899 the French composer Claude Debussy wrote three orchestral works which he grouped together and called "Noctumes," or "night songs." He presented them to his wife as a New Year's Day gift on

[1] Oscar Thompson, "Debussy: Man and Artist" (New York: Tudor Publishing Company, 1940)

the first of January, 1900. He said that he used the title "Nocturnes" in a "general and, more particularly, in a decorative sense," offering "all the various impressions and the special effects of light that the word suggests."

The first of the "Nocturnes" is titled "Clouds." The composer said that it "renders the changeless nature of the sky and the slow, solemn motion of the clouds, fading away in gray tones lightly tinged with white." The second nocturne, "Festivals," is described in detail in the following section. The third, and last of the group, is called "Sirens." It, according to Debussy, "depicts the sea and its countless rhythms. Eventually, among its moonlit silver waves the mysterious Sirens — those mythical persons, half-woman and half-bird, who lured mariners to their destruction by their seductive singing — are heard as they laugh and pass by."

Festivals

This is not a festival such as a carnival or fiesta where people are celebrating, for it takes place not on earth, but in the space surrounding the earth or in the imagination. Like a mirage, this musical festival is always just beyond us somewhere in the atmosphere. Here only light and sound exist, and quivering atoms are dancing the strange vibration that reflects flashes of light.

There is also the dazzling vision of a procession, one that passes through the festive scene and becomes part of it. The background, however, is always the same — an imaginative festival of light and color and tone, such as one might dream about but would never expect to experience — except in Debussy's music.

The composer has written:

> "'Festivals' gives us the vibrating atmosphere with sudden flashes of light. There is also the episode of the procession — a dazzling, fantastic vision — which passes through the festive scene and becomes merged in it. But the background remains always the same: the festival, with its belnding of music and luminous dust, participating in the cosmic rhythm."

"Festivals" opens brilliantly with a rhythmical, two-measure introduction:

Example 1

The English horn and clarinets play the first theme over a continuation of the rhythmical pattern of Example 1:

Example 2

After two measures in which the rhythm of Example 1 is heard very soft-ly by itself, the flutes and oboes play a modified version of Example 2. Another variant of Example 2 is then played by the bassoons and cellos.

Over a very loud, very low D-flat, the trumpets and trombones play a bold, rhythmical figure:

Example 3

After a harp glissando (a sliding of the fingers across the strings), the woodwinds play a figure in 15/8 meter:

Example 4

The strings take up an abbreviated form of Example 4, now in 9/8 meter, while the oboes and flutes play a melody which for two measures is similar to Example 2:

Example 5

Examples 4 and 5 are repeated in turn.
The French horns and bassoons play a bold figure:

Example 6

After three measures, the English horn plays an ascending passage which is answered by the oboes with a descending passage (Example 7). These measures are difficult to hear because of the texture of the music. Each of the two passages is repeated in turn.

Example 7

Two measures later, Example 6 appears in the upper strings; it is repeated by the lower strings.
The oboe introduces a new melody:

Example 8

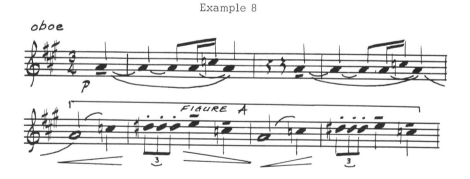

Example 8 is repeated by the flutes and clarinet.
Example 9, in the woodwinds against a rhythmical string accompaniment, is heard three times, continually growing louder.

Example 9

A sudden <u>pianissimo</u> (growing very soft) marks the repetition by the clarinets and bassoons of Figure A from Example 8. This is followed by a variant of Example 9 played by the oboes and English horn.

This alternation of Figure A from Example 8 with Example 9 is repeated twice, the first time softly, the second time loudly.

The insistent repetition of a triplet figure grows louder and louder.

Suddenly the orchestra is quiet except for a soft, rhythmical pulsation by pizzicato strings, harp and timpani. The approach "of the procession ... which passes through the festive scene" is heralded:

Example 10

The muted trumpets begin the fanfare theme of the procession:

Example 11

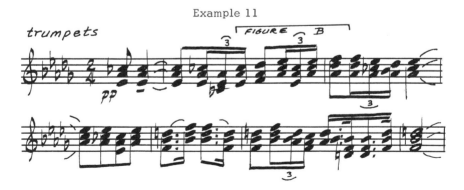

This is immediately repeated by the woodwinds. It gradually grows louder. The French horns and woodwinds alternately play a variant of Figure B from Example 11.

The military drum is heard with an insistent figure:

The trumpets and trombone play the fanfare theme, Example 11, while the violins and violas repeat a passage derived from Example 2; this mingling of the two themes suggests "the procession which passes through the festive scene and becomes merged in it. But the background remains persistently the same."

Suddenly the dynamic level decreases to a pianissimo and the flutes play a modified version of Example 2. This is repeated with a gradual crescendo.

The violins play a sustained melody that builds to a very loud climax:

Example 12

Again the dynamic level drops to a pianissimo; the figure of Example 4 (in 15/8 meter) is repeated. Example 5 is then heard in the flutes and oboes. Example 4 and 5 are repeated in succession.

A variant of Example 8 appears in the upper woodwinds over a pulsating figure in the strings and horns.

The fervor decreases and fragments of Example 8 appear in the bassoons and oboes, answered by fragments of the fanfare theme (Example 11) played by the flutes and brass.

The lower strings continue the pulsating rhythm, but the vitality seems to be waning. The merrymakers are gone and the festival-vision becomes only a memory.

A melancholy theme is played by the oboe and repeated by the flute:

Example 13

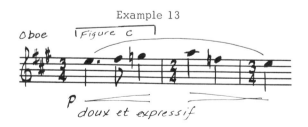

Figure C from Example 13 is repeated as follows:

oboe
bassoon
oboe
bassoon

In the twenty-measure <u>Coda</u> (the closing section) the music gradually fades away. The soft, rhythmical beating of a military drum is heard, leading to the final pizzicato chords in the lower strings.

> <u>Symphonic Poem</u> or <u>Tone Poem</u>: The symphonic poem, some-times called tone poem, is program music, since the form becomes a function of the program. Usually it is in a single movement, and sometimes parallels the sonata-allegro form, although the essential nature of a symphonic poem is its flexible treatment of melodic ideas.

Claude Debussy

(August 22, 1862 – March 25, 1918)

Claude Debussy was born in a suburb of Paris, the little village of St. Germain-en-Laye. His father owned a china shop there which went bank-rupt when Claude was three years old. The family then moved to Paris.

As a boy, Claude was interested in collecting butterflies and in paint-ing, but showed little talent for mus-ic. Fortunately his God-mother rec-ognized a hidden talent and encour-aged him to study the piano with a pupil of Frederic Chopin. By the time Claude was eleven, he was enrolled at the Paris Conservatory of Music where he studied for the next eleven years.

A cantata, "The Prodigal Son," won for the twenty-two year old De-bussy the Prix de Rome which entitled him to three years of study at the French Academy in Rome, Italy. The composer was most unhappy in Italy and left the Academy at the end of his second year. He returned to Paris and never moved very far away from that beloved city again.

Among his friends and acquaint-ances were many of the French "impressionistic" painters and "symbolist" poets. Frequently he would spend long hours in the cafes of the Montmartre section of Paris discussing art in general, and painting and poetry in particular.

As a composer, Debussy is best known for his orchestral works: "Nocturnes," "La Mer" ("The Sea"), "Prélude à l'Après-midi d'un faune " ("Prelude to the Afternoon of a Faun"), and "Images." His only completed opera, "Pelléas et Mélisande," is still widely performed. His many piano compositions are a delight for keyboard performers, and his only string quartet merits special mention. His many songs are not as widely performed as they once were, but are still a significant contribution to the singer's repertory.

THE PINES OF ROME

by Ottorino Respighi

The Italian composer, Ottorino Respighi, was inspired during his long residence in Rome to compose three major orchestral works commemorating the "Eternal City." In 1916 he wrote "The Fountains of Rome;" eight years later, in 1924, he completed "The Pines of Rome." The third and final work of this group, "Roman Carnivals," followed in 1928.

The style and texture of these compositions by Respighi are not as vague and fleeting as those of Claude Debussy. The Italian composer's purpose is much more definite, and it includes, by the very nature of the titles, a spirit of nationalism.

"In 'The Pines of Rome,'" the composer has said, "I use Nature as a point of departure in order to recall memories and visions. The century-old trees which dominate so characteristically the Roman landscape become testimony for the principal events in Roman life."[1]

In actuality, these Roman tone poems are programmatic symphonies, for they each consist of four contrasting movements similar in structure to the traditional symphonic format. "The Pines of the Appian Way" is the fourth movement of "The Pines of Rome," its finale.

The Pines of the Appian Way

In the year 312 B.C. the Roman emperor Appius Claudius Caecus built a road leading out of Rome to Brindisi, a port city on the Adriatic Sea and point of departure for ancient vessels sailing to classical Greece. This time-honored highway is known as the Appian Way.

The pines in the Roman countryside frequently grow in orderly rows by the side of the road, rather than in thick groves or clumps. The country-

[1] Letter of Respighi to Lawrence Gilman, quoted in Gilman's "Orchestral Music" (New York: Oxford University Press, 1951)

Photograph ENIT.

side itself is dreamy and quiet, a rolling plain with hills far off to the east. The Via Appia strikes through it, a reminder of the military empire that built it.

Remnants of the mighty Roman aqueduct may still be seen as one travels down this road, suggesting to the viewer some idea of their ancient splendor. For half the year the musty road, the columns of the aqueduct and the pines are shrouded in mist; for the other half, the hot, boiling sun beats down on them without mercy. This countryside has touched the imagination of countless generations who have stood there, recalling the marching feet of the ancient Roman soldiers, the magnficent chariots of their rulers.

The composer has written on the title-page of his score for "The Pines of Rome" a rather detailed description of what he tries to depict in "The Pines of the Appian Way":

> "Misty dawn on the Appian Way; solitary pine trees guarding the magic landscape; the muffled, ceaseless rhythm of unending footsteps. The poet has a fantastic vision of bygone glories. Trumpets sound, in the brilliance of the newly-risen sun, a consular army bursts forth toward the Sacred Way, mounting in triumph to the Capitol."

At first only the barely perceptible rhythm of the timpani is heard over strings marked pppp. (This rhythm or beat of the timpani never ceases until the movement is over.)

The misty dawn, the solitary loneliness of the undulating countryside is suggested by a melodic fragment played by the bass clarinet:

Example 1*

Always underneath this is the timpani, the "muffled, ceaseless rhythm of unending footsteps."

Faintly the French horns suggest the military legions of old:

Example 2

A hint of the fanfare to come is softly suggested by the clarinets:

Example 3

* © Copyright 1925 by G. Ricordi & C., Copyright Renewed 1953

"The magic landscape" which is guarded by "solitary pine trees" provides food and shelter for countless flocks of sheep. The tune of an ancient shepherd is suggested by an English horn solo of some fourteen measures. It begins:

Example 4

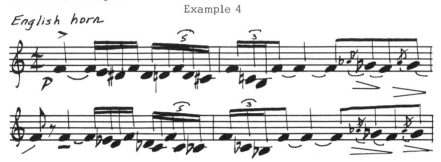

The bassoon and French horn repeat the fanfare theme, Example 3, softly. It is echoed by the clarinet and another French horn.

As from a distance, two trumpets play a variant of the fanfare:

Example 5

After Example 3 has been heard again in the winds, the distant trumpets play a variant of Example 5.

"The brilliance of a newly-risen sun" breaks forth as an unmuted trumpet loudly proclaims the fanfare theme, Example 3.

"A consular army bursts forth toward the Sacred Way," advancing brilliantly from this point to the end of the composition. Winds and upper strings play a loud, slowly ascending scale, over which the brass brilliantly play Example 6 (derived from previous thematic material).

Example 6

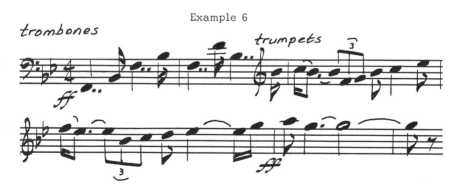

After a dynamic climax is reached, the brass take over the slow, sustained ascending scale, while, from the depths of the orchestra, the tubas proclaim Example 5.

The drive of the timpani beat is incessant; the dynamic climaxes come closer together, each one more brilliant than its predecessor. Theme overlaps theme as "trumpets sound ... a fantastic vision of bygone glories." The consular army bursts forth, ... mounting in triumph to the Capitol."

Ottorino Respighi

(July 9, 1879 - April 18, 1936)

Ottorino Respighi was born of a musical family; his grandfather had been a choir director for the churches of Bologna, and his father was a pianist and teacher at the Bologna School of Music. It was only natural that after piano lessons from his father, young Ottorino should be enrolled in his twelfth year at the School of Music. At the same time, he was also taking violin lessons.

At nineteen Respighi started the study of composition. For two years he took lessons in his native Bologna, then he went to Russia and became a pupil of Rimsky-Korsakov in both composition and orchestration. This was followed by studies in Berlin with Max Bruch.

Bettmann Archive.

His training completed, Respighi started his career as a concert violinist. In 1913 he was appointed instructor in composition at the Santa Cecilia Academy in Rome. He fell so in love with this city that he resided in Rome the rest of his life. The villa that he built for his family he called "I Pini" ("The Pines").

As a composer Respighi is best known for his three orchestral works inspired by his adopted city of Rome, "The Fountains of Rome," " Roman Carnivals " and the third, " The Pines of Rome." Although he composed several operas, they are no longer produced. He also wrote ballets, cantatas, symphonies, chamber music and songs.

SYMPHONY NO. 6

"The Pastoral"

by Ludwig van Beethoven

In great contrast to the rather specific "program" of Respighi's "Pines" is the "Scene by the Brook" from Beethoven's Symphony No. 6. In this latter work the composer attempts to present, to quote him:

> "no realistic picture, but something in which the emotions are expressed which are aroused in one by the pleasures of the country. People will not require titles to recognize the general intention to be more a matter of feeling thab of painting in sounds. All painting in instrumental music, if pushed too far, is a failure. The hearers should be allowed to discover for themselves the intent."

Beethoven subtitled his Symphony No. 6 "The Pastoral: A Recollection of Rural Life." The five movements each have a descriptive title of their own: (1) "Awakening of cheerful emotions on arriving in the country"; (2) "Scene by the Brook"; (3) "Peasants' Merry-Making"; (4) "Thunderstorm - Tempest"; and (5) "Shepherd's Hymn."

All his life Beethoven had been fascinated by the countryside, by nature, by the lush growth of trees that formed the beautiful Vienna Woods near his home. His long walks down shaded paths became more frequent as his hearing grew worse and he approached total deafness. Embarrassed to say to friends, "Shout, speak louder for I am deaf," because he felt they expected a musician to have a better sense of hearing than the average person rather than less or none, he became more contemplative and communed more with nature than with his fellow man.

"No one loves country life as I do," Beethoven wrote to a friend. "It is as if every tree and bush could understand my silent questions and respond to them." Shortly after he had composed "The Pastoral" the composer wrote to another friend, "When you wander through the mysterious forests of pine, remember that Beethoven often made poetry there — or, as they say, 'composed.'"

Toward the end of his life, Beethoven took a walk through the countryside near his home in Heiligenstadt, a rural suburb of Vienna, with a friend, Anton Schindler. As they strolled through a meadow, they found a brook bordered by tall, stately elms. "Beethoven stopped repeatedly," Schindler later wrote, "and let his glance, full of blissful feelings, wander over the beautiful landscape. Then, seating himself upon the grass and leaning against an elm, he asked me whether there was no yellow-breasted bunting to be heard in the tops of the trees. But all was still. H then told me, 'Here I composed the "Scene by the Brook" and those

yellow-breasted buntings up there, the quail, nightingales and cuckoos round about, composed with me.'"

Second Movement: "Scene by the Brook"

The French composer, Hector Berlioz, has suggested that "Beethoven, without doubt, created this admirable movement while reclining on the grass, his eyes uplifted, ears intent, fascinated by the thousand varying hues of light and sound, looking and listening at the same time to the scintillating ripple of the brook that breaks its waves over the pebbles of its shores."

This is music of contemplation. In listening to it, it is well to remember the composer's remark that this is not a realistic picture of a scene by the brook. Rather, it is "something in which the emotions are expressed which are aroused in one by the pleasure of the country." Except for the calls of the birds in its closing measures — the quail, the nightingale and the cuckoo — one does not hear imitative sounds in this movement.

The serene, peaceful countryside — perhaps even the gentle meandering of the brook — is suggested by the dreamy, flowing accompaniment heard at the very beginning played by some of the strings:

Example 1

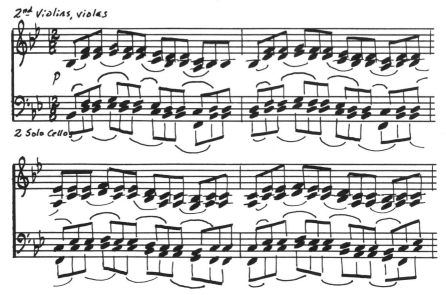

Over this accompaniment, the first violins play a gentle melody:

Example 2

Example 2 is repeated by clarinet and bassoon, accompanied by a variant of Example 1.

This leads directly into Example 3, which is introduced by the violins. In the third measure, the clarinet starts to imitate the violins while the violins continue on with their melody.

Example 3

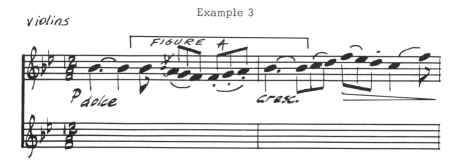

After a very short transition passage, a variant of Example 2 is played by the violins over an accompaniment derived from Example 1.

A haunting melody, Example 4, is introduced by the bassoon which is joined in the second measure by the violas and two solo cellos. It is continued by the violins which are later joined by a flute.

Example 4

The flute and violins repeat Example 4.

Figure A from Example 3 is heard three times in succession as follows:

> violas and solo cellos
> violins
> flute and oboe

The flowing theme suggestive of the brook, Example 1, is implied by the clarinets and bassoons.

A new melody is started by the violins and violas, and completed by the flute:

Example 5

Example 2 returns in the oboe; it is continued in varied form by the flute and oboe.

Figure A from Example 3 is played by the violas and solo cellos. It is then taken up by the violins and then by the flute.

The clarinet enters with Example 2, which continues in altered form.

begins as the flute enters with Example 2.

After another short transition passage, the melody of Example 4 returns again in the bassoon, joined in the second measure by violas and cellos. Example 4 is repeated by the oboe and violins.

Once again the violas and solo cellos play Figure A which is imitated first by the violins, then by the oboe.

For a few measures, only the rhythm derived from Example 2 is heard. Then come the songs of the birds — the nightingale (flute), the quail (the oboe), and the cuckoo (the clarinet):

Example 6

This four-measure phrase ends with Figure A from Example 3. The bird songs are repeated. Repetitions of Figure A conclude the movement.

Ludwig van Beethoven

(December 16, 1770 - March 26, 1827)

When Ludwig van Beethoven was born, in a tiny garret apartment in Bonn, he seemed predestined to follow in his forebears' footsteps and become a professional musician. To this end, his father started the boy's

lessons at the keyboard at an early age and required him to spend long hours practising. By the time Ludwig was thirteen, he was appointed pianist for the court opera orchestra, and a year later accepted the post of assistant organist for his church at an annual salary of about $63.

At twenty-two, Beethoven moved to Vienna, then the capital of the music world. He made that city his home for the balance of his life. For many years the Viennese public knew him only as a piano soloist, as his compositions were not widely performed at first. The composer was always in grave financial straits and moved from one inexpensive lodging to another. He encountered difficulty with his hearing, and, by the time he was 49, he was totally deaf. Undaunted, he continued to compose.

Chapter VIII

COMPOSERS AND FOLK MUSIC

Most people are familiar with the expressions <u>folk songs</u> and <u>folk music</u>, yet it is not an easy task to define these terms.

In general, folk music is very old. It is passed from one generation to the next by oral tradition. In its original setting, folk music is not written down. Because of this, songs and their texts develop many variants, and it is now impossible to determine the original form of any given folk song.

Folk music could originate anywhere at any time, but it was usually created by the more rural civilizations, and by untrained, non-professional musicians. It was performed by singers and players with very little, if any, musical training.

Although many folk songs originated to accompany work — perhaps on a sailing vessel or in a cotton field — many songs evolved strictly for entertainment purposes. Folk music is actually the expression of a whole people or tribe, or at least of an important segment of a culture.

Composers have been affected both consciously and unconsciously by the great literature of folk music. In the works of this chapter you will discover how three different composers have made use of this heritage. In the first composition, the "Afro-American Symphony" of William Grant Still, only the style of a folk music is to be discovered; no folk songs or folk themes are employed. Ralph Vaughan Williams, in the second work of this chapter, quotes entire folk tunes in his "English Folk Song Suite." A middle ground is reached by Johannes Brahms in his "Academic Festi-val Overture," the final work of this chapter. Brahms quotes goodly portions of four folk songs, yet develops them in an art form that is strictly Brahmsian in flavor and technique.

These three composers represent three different cultural and ethnic backgrounds. William Grant Still is an American who has been influenced both by the main stream of the art and folk music of the United States, and, more specifically, by the heritage of the black American tradition, including <u>blues</u> and <u>jazz</u>. Ralph Vaughan Williams was an Englishman, and spent many years collecting and editing the carols and folk songs of Great Britain. Johannes Brahms represents the Germanic tradition, for he was born in Hamburg. He arranged countless German folk songs for both choruses and vocal soloists.

Perhaps the best "history" of folk singing is a brief one stated by

Ralph Vaughan Williams, one of the composers represented in this chapter. He said:

> "In primitive times before there were newspapers to tell us the news, history books to teach us the past, and novels to excite our imagination, all these things had to be done by the ballad singer, who naturally had to do it all from memory. To this end he cast what he had to tell into a metrical form and thus the ballad stanza arose. As a further aid to memory and to add to the emotional value of what he had to say, he added musical notes to his words, and it is from this that the ordinary folk tune of four strains arose. Folk music, you must always remember, is an applied art. The idea of art for art's sake has happily no place in the primitive (mind)."[1]

AFRO-AMERICAN SYMPHONY

by William Grant Still

Proud of the fact that he is an American, William Grant Still believes that every American composer should be well acquainted with jazz no matter how much or how little of it he uses in his compositions, for "jazz is one of the few idioms developed by the United States that can be said to belong to no other people on earth." Proud, too, of his black heritage, Still early in life decided to use appropriate titles for many of his compositions and to embody in his works the distinctive features of black music.

The very first words printed in the conductor's score of the "Afro-American Symphony" indicate the composer's profoundly religious nature: "With humble thanks to God, the source of inspiration." It is Still's philosophy that, "he who develops his God-given gifts with a view to aiding humanity, manifests truth."

The "Afro-American Symphony" was composed in 1930 and first performed by the Rochester Philharmonic Orchestra in 1931 under the baton of Howard Hanson, who later conducted the work in Berlin, Stuttgart and Leipzig. The audience in Berlin broke a twenty-year tradition to encore the Scherzo; later an audience in Budapest did the same thing when Karl Krueger conducted the symphony there.

"At the time this symphony was written," Still says, "no thought was given to a program for the 'Afro-American Symphony,' the program being added after the completion of the work. I have regretted this step because in this particular instance a program is decidedly inadequate. The

[1] Ralph Vaughan Williams, "National Music" (London: Oxford University Press, 1934)

88

program devised at that time stated that the music portrayed the 'sons of the soil,' that is that it offered a composite musical portrait of those Afro-Americans who have not responded completely to the cultural influences of today. It is true that an interpretation of that sort may be read into the music. Nevertheless, one who hears it is quite sure to discover other meanings which are probably broader in their scope. He may find the piece portrays four distinct types of Afro-Americans whose sole relationship is the physical one of dark skins. On the other hand, he may find that the music offers the sorrows and joys, the struggles and achievement of an individual Afro-American. Also it is quite probable that the music will speak to him of moods peculiar to colored Americans. Unquestionably, various other interpretations may be read into the music.

"Each movement of this Symphony presents a definite emotion, excerpts from poems of Paul Laurence Dunbar being included in the score for the purpose of explaining these emotions. Each movement has a suggestive title: the first is "Longing," the second "Sorrow," the third "Humor," and the fourth "Sincerity." In it, I have stressed an original motive in the blues idiom, employed as the principal theme of the first movement, and appearing in various forms in the succeeding movements, where I have tried to present it in characteristic manner.

"The 'Afro-American Symphony' represent(s) the Negro of the days not far removed from the Civil War.

"When judged by the laws of musical form, the Symphony is somewhat irregular. This irregularity is in my estimation justified since it has no ill effect on the proportional balance of the composition. Moreover, when one considers that an architect is free to design new forms of buildings, and bears in mind the freedom permitted creators in other fields of art, he can hardly deny a composer the privilege of altering established forms as long as the sense of proportion is justified."[1]

Third Movement: Animato

The third movement of a symphony since the days of Beethoven has traditionally been called the Scherzo, an Italian word meaning a joke, jest or trick. This is an apt designation for this movement since the composer has stated that its suggestive subtitle is "Humor, expressed through religious fervor."

In the score Still quotes the following lines of the great black poet Paul Laurence Dunbar (1872-1906) for the third movement:

> "An' we'll shout ouah halleluyahs,
> On dat mighty reck'nin' day."

"The harmonies employed in the Symphony," the composer states, "are quite conventional except in a few places. The use of this style of harmonization was necessary in order to attain the simplicity and to intensi-

[1] William Grant Still quoted in "Studies in Contemporary American Music: William Grant Still" by Verna Arvey (New York: J. Fischer & Bros., 1939)

fy in music those qualities which enable the hearer to recognize it as Negro music. The orchestration was planned with a view to the attainment of effective simplicity."

The tempo indication of the Scherzo is <u>Animato</u>, ♩ = 126. The brief introduction (some seven measures in length) is based on variants of Figure A of the Principal Theme, Example 2. A timpani roll is heard; the motive of Figure A is played first by low winds and strings:

Example 1*

The violins take up the Principal Theme of the movement; the tenor banjo is prominent in the accompaniment.

Example 2

Strings and clarinets play a variant of Example 2, accompanied by a syncopated figure in the upper woodwinds.

The second theme, Example 3, is derived from the Principal Theme, Example 2; it is played by the upper woodwinds and strings reinforced at times by the trumpet.

Example 3

The dynamic level subsides; the oboe, over a pizzicato string accompaniment, plays the Principal Theme, Example 2, in a saucy manner. The flutes start to play it, but quickly abandon the theme.

In a transitional passage, the trombones are prominent:

* Copyright 1930 by William Grant Still; quoted by permission of William Grant Still

Example 4

An ascending passage of four measures for strings and woodwinds, growing in dynamic intensity, is heard.

In the following measures, a "call and answer" pattern is established between the combined strings and woodwinds, and the brass. (It is based, rhythmically, on the second variant of Figure A from Example 1.)

Example 5

The "call and answer" idea is carried on between the low woodwinds and strings, and the low brass.

A melodic variant of Example 2 is started by the flutes and continued by the oboe. Soon the strings take up a motive derived from Figure B of Example 2.

The muted trumpets, in a rhythmic passage, are heard with a variant of Figure A from Example 2; they are answered by the other brass. The full orchestra then takes up the antiphonal "call and answer" pattern; this passage is based on Figure B from Example 2.

The dynamic level subsides; violins play a melodic variant of Example 2. (The banjo is prominent in the accompaniment throughout this section.) Next, the woodwinds play their variant of Example 2.

The violins are now heard with Example 3.

A bridge passage leads to the Coda; it is based on a variant of Figure C from Example 4.

The strings, fortissimo, play a syncopated melodic variant of Example 2; the trumpets accompany this with a trasnformation of the "blues theme" from the first movement of the Symphony.

That combination, Example 6, starts out:

Example 6

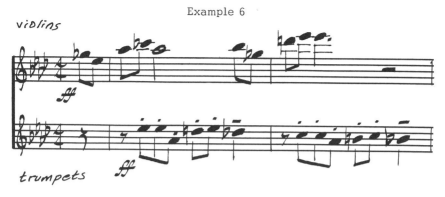

The music quickly builds to a dynamic climax; the brief Scherzo is then over.

William Grant Still

(May 11, 1896 -   )

William Grant Still was born in Woodville, Mississippi. Both his parents were accredited teachers and musicians; both were talented and brilliant. His father's musical education on the cornet had been gained by making a seventy-five mile trip for each lesson! Later, his father founded and conducted a brass band in Woodville, the only one in town. He also tried his hand at composition. Unfortunately, he died when William was six months old.

William's mother then took him with her to Little Rock, Arkansas , where she obtained a job teaching school. About five years later she married a postal employee, Charles B. Shepperson, who was a fan of operatic music. He spent a large share of his meagre income buying phonograph records of arias performed by the outstanding stars of that period. This gave young William an opportunity to hear music that pleased him more than any he had heard before.

At sixteen William graduated from high school as first honor bearer and class valedictorian. When the question of college arose, his mother tried to steer him away from a course in music composition, for she felt that there was no future for a serious musician, especially a black one. He therefore enrolled at Wilberforce University where he took a Bachelor of Science degree. Nevertheless, he played in the university string quartet and made arrangements for their band. The first concert of his compositions was a recital which he gave at Wilberforce.

Within two months of graduation, Still left the University. Lean days followed. He married, worked at odd jobs, played oboe and cello with various orchestras, starved, froze, joined the United States Navy. All this time he wondered how he could continue his professional study of music. Through a legacy from his father, he studied at Oberlin College in Ohio. Then, because of the merit of his work, he was given a scholarship to study composition privately.

W. C. Handy, the "father of the blues," gave Still his first job as an arranger. He toured with Handy's Band from New York through the South. Now that he could afford it, Still applied to study composition with George W. Chadwick who, because of Still's talent, wanted to teach him free of charge. A scholarship from the revolutionary Franco-American composer Edgar Varese to study with him followed.

Still then played in pit orchestras for vaudeville and New York musicals. He played banjo in the orchestra of the Plantation Nightclub on Broadway. When its conductor left, he advance to that position. When CBS started, Still was arranging for the network broadcasts, and, later, turned to NBC as an arranger for the Maxwell House Hour. When its conductor left, some of the men in the orchestra suggested that Still become their conductor. The management agreed and William Grant Still became the first black to conduct an all-white orchestra in New York.

William Grant Still is known for five symphonies (including the "Afro-American Symphony"), a quantity of orchestral works, pieces for band, compositions for the accordian and a number of piano solos. He has composed six operas, some on Negro themes. His catalogue of works includes numorous songs and works for chorus. Of his four ballets, "Sahdji" is the best known.

ENGLISH FOLK SONG SUITE

by Ralph Vaughan Williams

The folk songs of his native England fascinated Ralph Vaughan Williams all of his life. He joined a folk song society for the first time in 1904; in 1911 he became one of the founding members of the then new English Folk Dance Society, and in 1921 became one of its Vice-Presidents. During World War I he lectured for the Society at summer schools, conducted festivals of folk songs, and joined in the folk dancing. According to his wife, Vaughan Williams "considered it of the first importance for the musical well-being of the country that this inheritance of song and dance should become a part of every child's life."[1]

The composer claimed that folk music was "sincere music which has withstood the test of time, music which must be representative of our race as no other music can. ... At the root of the musical quality of a nation lies the natural music whose simplest and clearest manifestation is the folk song."[2]

The public supported this renaissance of folk music and dance. Classes were offered in colleges and universities to train teachers in it, and the public and private schools searched for adequate materials for their glee clubs and choruses. "New arrangements were called for, piano accompaniments or choral settings," writes Mrs. Vaughan Williams. "Because he knew and loved the music, Ralph was adept at providing them. Folk music weaves in and out of his work all through his life, sometimes adapted for some particular occasion, sometimes growing into the fabric of orchestral writing. One such work, the suite "English Folk Songs," was written for the Royal Military School of Music. ... This had been one of the works he had been particularly happy to undertake, as he enjoyed working in a medium new to him. A military band was a change from an orchestra, and in his not-so-far-off Army days (he had served in combat in World War I) he had heard enough of the 'ordinary ... light stuff' to feel that a chance to play real tunes would be an agreeable ... experience for the bandsmen."

When the suite was completed in 1923, it was so well received by both performers and public, Vaughan Williams was encouraged to allow someone to arrange it for symphony orchestra. This he was happy to do; he allowed Gordon Jacob to transcribe the work for full orchestra.

The "English Folk Song Suite" is in three movements: March, Intermezzo and March. Each part is a collection of folk songs intertwined without any real attempt at development.

March: "Folk Songs from Somerset"

The second March of the Suite, the last of the three movements, is subtitled "Folk Songs from Somerset." Somerset is a county of more than a thousand square miles in southwest England, a hilly country of fertile valleys long used for pasturing dairy cattle and growing fruit. Somerset is closely associated with King Alfred and the legend of King Arthur and the Knights of the Round Table. The town of Bath is one of its principal cities, famous as an eighteenth-century watering place; it contains ruins dating back to the time of the Roman occupation of England.

In this March, Vaughan Williams makes use of four folk songs from the Somerset area: "Blow Away the Morning Dew," "High Germany," "Tree So High" and "John Barleycorn." The composer takes the traditional form

[1] Ursula Vaughan Williams, "R. V. W. : A Biography of Ralph Vaughan Williams (London: Oxford University Press, 1964)
[2] Ralph Vaughan Williams, op. cit.

of a march and incorporates these four tunes as its themes.

A march is a compound form. Its larger structure consists of three parts: a march, a trio, amd a repetition of the march. The march is in ternary form, while the trio is in binary form. Notice, as you listen to this movement, how Vaughan Williams has used the traditional form, simply incorporating the folk songs in place of original themes.

A four measure introduction is played by the woodwinds.

A clarinet begins the first part of the tune, "Blow Away the Morning Dew"; it is joined later by flutes and trumpets.

Eaxample 1*

The second part of the tune follows immediately; it begins:

* "English Folk Song Suite" by Ralph Vaughan Williams, Copyright 1924 by Boosey & Co., Ltd.; Renewed 1951. Reprinted by permission of Boosey & Hawkes, Inc.

Example 2

A modal tune (based on the scale of <u>E</u> to <u>E</u> using only the white keys, known as the <u>Phrygian mode</u>) known as "High Germany" is played by bassoon, horn, violins and violas. It begins:

Example 3

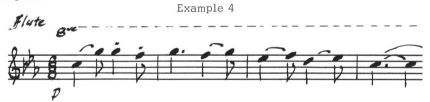

The tune of "Blow Away the Morning Dew" returns. Example 1 is heard once; Example 2 is played twice to conclude the March section.

A march rhythm is established by the orchetsra, in which the military drums are prominent; this introduces the Trio.

The tune, "Tree So High," is played by flute and clarinet. Pizzicato strings and military drum are heard in the accompaniment. The tune begins:

Example 4

The melody of "John Barleycorn" follows immediately, played boldly by the trombones. It begins:

Example 5

The entire Trio section is repeated.

The first section, the March, is repeated in its entirety just as it was heard the first time.

<u>Modes</u>: A mode is a set of notes which forms the material of the melodic idiom of a composition. In the eighteenth and nineteenth centuries, only two principal modes were used in art music, the <u>Ionian</u> and the <u>Aeolian</u>, known more commonly as the <u>major</u> and <u>minor</u> scales. However, from the Middle Ages onward, many other patterns were in use. Many folk songs in popular use today are modal in nature. These Medieval modes can best be described by using scales built on only the white keys of the piano. They include the <u>Dorian</u> mode (D to D), the <u>Phrygian</u> mode (E to E), the <u>Lydian</u> mode (F to F), and the <u>Mixolydian</u> mode (G to G), as well as many others.

Ralph Vaughan Williams

(October 12, 1872 – August 26, 1958)

Ralph Vaughan Williams was born in Down Ampney in the English county of Gloucestershire; he was the son of a clergyman. He received his early education at the Charterhouse School in London, and then attended the Royal College of Music for two years. He completed his Bachelor of Music degree at Trinity College, Cambridge.

After finishing school in his early twenties, he became a church organist for three years. Wishing to do additional work in the field of composition, he went to Berlin to study with composer Max Bruch. He returned from the continent to complete his Doctor of Music degree at Cambridge in 1901.

Late in emerging as a composer, it was perhaps joining the English Folk Song Society that gave him the inspiration to start writing, for he composed one of his first important works that year, "In the Fen Country." This was followed by a survey of folk music from the Norfolk area and the composition of "Three Norfolk Rhapsodies."

Besides nine symphonies, Vaughan Williams is remembered for his six operas, many successful cantatas — mostly of a religious nature — his "Serenade to Music," "Job: A Masque for Dancing," several concertos including one for tuba, and a quantity of chamber music.

ACADEMIC   FESTIVAL   OVERTURE

by Johannes Brahms

An honorary degree, that of Doctor of Music, was offered to Brahms in 1876 by Cambridge University. The invitation stated that, "England has thus the opportunity of making recognition of your high services to art in which all earnest musicians will concur." At first the composer was pleased by the honor, writing to a friend that he was "extremely delighted with this great adventure."

Then he had second thoughts. The University would not confer the degree unless Brahms appeared for the ceremonies in person. Troubled with sea-sickness, the composer dreaded the thought of crossing the rough English channel. He also disliked traveling in a foreign country where he could neither speak nor read the language. Since he placed so little value on worldly honors and titles, he decided against the trip and refused the degree.

Three years later the University of Breslau in his native Germany voted to confer on him the honorary degree of Doctor of Philosophy, since they considered Brahms the "leader , in Germany, of music of the serious or-der." This time the composer acknowledged the honor by mailing a post-card to a friend of his on the University faculty, asking that his gratitude be expressed to the professors. A year past. Finally Brahms agreed to come to Breslau to receive the degree; he then discovered that the Uni-versity expected him to "express his gratitude" in musical form.

That summer, while enjoying a holiday at the lakeside village of Ischl in the Austrian Alps — "there is a different air and a different life here," he wrote — he composed a concert overture in which he made use of four college songs as themes. At first he called his composition "Viadrina," a Latin name for the University of Breslau. Later he changed it to its present title, the "Academic Festival Overture."

Brahms described the work as "a very boisterous potpourri of student songs." In January of 1881 the composer conducted the first performance at the concert hall in Breslau. The Rector, the Senate and the members of the faculty of the School of Philosophy sat in the front rows. There were murmurings and the shaking of heads among them about this new composition, for the composer had used a couple of student drinking songs heard frequently in the local taverns! Nevertheless, these songs represent the esteem in which, at heart, those students held their alma mater.

The music opens, indeed, in the tavern, "with a tune immediately as-sociated with beer-mugs." The tempo is marked <u>Allegro</u>; the tune is played by the violins over a string and low woodwind accompaniment marked pianissimo:

Example 1

After this theme is developed briefly, a new theme — almost like a part-song or choral — is introduced. It is slow and sustained; it begins:

Example 2

The first theme returns briefly.
A bold theme, Example 3, interrupts the progress of the music.

Example 3

A bridge passage leads to the introduction of the first of the four student songs which Brahms used, "We Have Built a Stately House." The French horns proclaim this part-song which begins:

Example 4

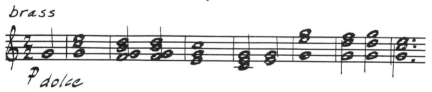

It is expanded and leads to a dynamic climax, at which point the composer marks the score L'istesso tempo, un poco maestoso ("the same tempo, but more majestic"). The full orchestra takes up Example 5 which is derived from Example 1:

Example 5

Melodic fragments from both Examples 1 and 5 follow in a very brief development.

The second violins, against pizzicato cellos, then take up the second student song, "The Father of Our Country":

Example 6

Instead of developing this theme, Example 6, the most ribald touch of the "Overture" follows. A song which ridicules freshmen, "What Comes Down from the Hills," is introduced by the humorous sounds of the bassoon, later joined by the oboe. Marked <u>Animato</u>, it begins:

Example 7

Example 7 builds to a climax, and, after an episode, it is repeated. Then some of the themes are recapitulated. Suggestions of the opening section are heard, then the full orchestra takes up Example 3 boldly. Next Example 1 is heard, then a variant of Example 5 is played by the upper woodwinds and strings. This is followed by Example 4 in altered form. The more expressive Example 6 follows, again played by the second violins. Once again the humorous Example 7 interrupts, building to a dynamic climax.

At that climax, the tempo changes to <u>Maestoso</u>, ♩= ♪ ("majestic"); the tonality changes to C major. The historic, Medieval Latin student song, "Gaudeamus Igitur" ("Let Us Rejoice") is introduced:

Example 8

Woodwinds, brass

This tune continues to build to one dynamic climax after another up to the conclusion of the "Overture," shouting — as it were — the Medieval melody which suggests all the joys of student life.

Johannes Brahms

(May 7, 1833 – April 3, 1897)

Johannes Brahms was born of an extremely poor family who lived in the slum area of Hamburg, Germany. His father was a double bass player in the local theater orchestra; his mother earned additional money for the family by taking in sewing.

At thirteen Brahms accepted his first porition as a professional musician, playing in the local taverns for dancing. Soon he obtained an additional position playing the backstage piano for the local theater. Through a friend of his father's, he was able to spend two summers away from Hamburg at the little town of Winsen, where he conducted the male chorus of the village and tried his hand at composition. Johannes arranged a number of folk songs for male voices in addition to the creation of some original work.

When he was seventeen, Brahms had the good fortune to meet the famous Hungarian violinist Remenyi, who requested the young lad to join him on his concert tour as piano accompanist. During these travels, Brahms met Franz Liszt in Weimar, Robert Schumann at Düsseldorf (after this meeting Schumann made an entry in his diary, "Brahms to see me — a genius!") and Hector Berlioz at Leipzig.

Late in emerging as a composer, Brahms did not write his first symphony until he was forty. This was followed by three more equally artistic symphonies. He is also known for his "German Requiem," many fine piano compositions, concertos, and two overtures, the "Academic Festival Overture" and the "Tragic Overture."

His art songs for solo voice are among his most important compositions. These include a number of settings of German folk songs.

Chapter IX

JAZZ

One of the most important musical developments in modern world history was caused by the largely forced migration of great numbers of African Negroes to the various parts of the Americas. These slaves, most of whom came from West Africa, brought with them the heritage of a highly developed and important folk music. In Africa they had known a wide variety of instruments, and there had been "professional musicians" in many of the tribes. They had music for a wide assortment of activities, including entertainment. For example, the Bahutu of Ruanda had at least twenty-four different types of social songs, including, according to one authority, "those played by professional musicians for entertainment, songs for beer drinking, war homage to a chief, hunting, harvesting, and general work; songs sung at the birth of a child or to admonish erring members of the society, to recount a successful elephant hunt, to deride Europeans; songs of death, vulgar songs, and others."[1]

Work songs were common, too. The Watusi, also of Ruanda, whose civilization centered around the breeding of cattle, had "songs in praise of cows, songs to indicate the importance of having cows, songs for taking cattle home in the evening, ... for drawing water for cattle," and so on.

Once in the United States, these black slaves were affected by the music of their white masters. From them they learned some songs; others they learned from missionaries or from neighbors in the cities. Some of these songs "were sung in styles indistinguishable from those of the whites, but on most of them the Negroes imposed some stylistic traits from Africa. They presumably also continued to sing African songs and to compose new songs in the African styles, but this was problematic because the slaves did not have a common language and tribal groups were purposely broken up by the slave traders."[2]

Perhaps the most important element of their heritage from Africa was the sense of rhythm; they frequently used percussion instruments in a

[1] Alan P. Merriam, "African Music" in "Continuity and Change in African Cultures" edited by William Bascom and Melville J. Herskovits (Chicago : University of Chicago Press, 1959)
[2] Bruna Nettle, "Folk and Traditional Music of the Western Continents" (Englewood Cliffs: Prentice-Hall, Inc., 1965)

rhythmic accompaniment. A second influence was the call-and-response pattern of many of the African songs, with a leader asking a question in the song while the chorus replied. The Africans loved instruments, and this probably led the early slaves to devise inexpensive instruments of their own: the washtub or gutbucket, washboards used as scrapers and placed on baskets for resonance; frying pans, cowbells, bottles, wood or bone clappers. They also quickly adopted and adapted a variety of European-devised instruments, including the harmonica, banjo, fiddles and brass instruments.

No less a person than Thomas Jefferson said that "in music, the Blacks are more generally gifted than the Whites, with accurate ears for tune and time, and they have been found capable of imagining (composing) a small catch. Whether they will be equal to the composition of a more extensive run of melody, or of complicated harmony, is yet to be proved."

The spiritual is, to a large extent, a borrowing from the rural southern whites. The songs of the blacks were frequently identical in text and melody with the "white spirituals" sung in the southern mountain regions, but they were sung by the blacks in a different manner, with a more rhythmical accompaniment, and, frequently, with improvisations in the melodic line.

The blues may be related to these spirituals. The so-called field blues were simply short calls and wails, repeated by field hands communicating with each other in the cotton fields. As in Africa, so in the United States individual song makers have come forth to create original songs out of a style already in existence. Perhaps the first great "blues composer" was Leadbelly — whose real name was Huddie Ledbetter (1888-1949), a Texas convict. The typical form of his song — also adopted by the early jazz bands that played the blues — was three part: the first two parts were similar in content, both musically and textually, while the third part was in contrast. This form can be observed in the "St. Louis Blues," for example.

A frequent characteristic of the blues is the flattened or slightly lowered, third and seventh degrees of the major scale. The origin of this practise is unknown. It is also typical of the blues that the main melody have short phrases, separated by pauses, long enough for an answering countermelody, as in the call-and-answer patterns of the tribal ceremonies of West Africa.

Jazz is a style created by obscure American musicians, predominantly black. Because most of this music is improvised, or created while being performed, the names of the performers are better known than those of the composers.

Jazz musicians do not play each other's compositions faithfully from the printed page of notes as concert performers of European art music do. Jazz improvisation resembles many Asiatic and African traditions, with a give-and-take between drummer and melody-players.

While jazz is an American product, representing a fusion of West African and European musical habits, it is difficult to trace its history. Because, as has been pointed out, jazz is largely improvisation, its history can only be traced in performance through phonograph records. Since these are rare before 1923, and non-existent before 1917, the origins of jazz are obscure. Jelly Roll Morton — whose real name was Ferdinand Morton (1885-1942) — claimed he invented jazz in New Orleans in 1902. This boast is denied by all other participants in its development. At any rate, he was the first great jazz musician of whom we have direct knowledge, and he has established a date that gives us some idea of when jazz evolved.

Jazz is basically an art of performance. Because of this, its history is basically a catalogue of performers. In contrast to a symphony or sonata which sounds about the same no matter who happens to perform it, a jazz piece has a marked difference each time it is performed. For example, a present-day recording by Duke Ellington of his "Black and Tan Fantasy" will differ quite a bit from his band's original 1927 version simply because the group's personnel has changed. The soloists are not the same. The overall structure doesn't differ from one performance to the next, but the timbre, the emotional interpretation, the very melodic lines of the breaks or solos themselves differ. This is why a performance by Count Basie's orchestra of the "St. Louis Blues" is something very different from Louis Armstrong's recorded interpretation of the same piece. The whole character of one group is simply very different from that of the other!

A principal characteristic of jazz is its reliance on improvisation. Improvisation in jazz can take many forms. Sometimes there is an elaborate, on-the-spot series of variations on a tune or set of chords. Sometimes it is only a subtle hint of extemporization: a slight change of note value here, a small change of emphasis there.

Jazz is also a social phenomenon. Its origins are closely tied to the migration of blacks from the plantations to the cities of the South. This was occasioned by the boll-weevil plague that hit the cotton fields.

The development of jazz was fostered by the successful use of music in the fabled Storeyville district of New Orleans, a series of nightspots and gambling halls. Jazz moved to Chicago when the United States Navy ordered Storeyville closed during World War I. The number of speakeasies or illegal nightclubs in Chicago after the Eighteenth Amendment, forbidding alcoholic beverages, was passed provided a ready market for jazz entertainment. The emergence of jazz in New York City, at first in Harlem and later in downtown Manhattan, was closely tied in with the first major commercial exploitation of this form of music.

The development of the phonograph, and the later popularity of movies and television, helped make jazz known in the farthest corners of the United States, and even across the oceans.

ST. LOUIS BLUES

by W. C. Handy

The blues is one of the early forms of jazz. The name itself is fairly self-destructive. Ever since Elizabethan times, to "have the blues" has meant a state of sadness and despondency. And Negro blues have usually been sad songs about loneliness or bad times, about the jinx which brings bad luck, the lover who gets betrayed, the good times and the evil days. The first blues singers are unknown by name, but we know their professions: cotton-pickers, stevedores, railroad men. For them the blues became an emotional release, a way of facing up to life by singing about it.

The form of the blues is simple enough: a first line that is repeated, followed by a third line that rhymes — more or less — with the other two:

> If you see me comin', hoist your window high,
> Oh, if you see me comin', hoist your window high,
> And if you see me goin', hang your head and cry.

The stanza is usually sung to a twelve-bar chordal pattern, although once in a while they could be eight or sixteen bars long. For many years after the blues first became popular, this twelve-bar form served as the basis for all jazz. One of the earliest twelve-bar patterns sounds like this:

Example 1

[musical notation: six measures numbered 1-6, grand staff]

[musical notation: six measures numbered 7-12, grand staff]

W. C. Handy is the best known name among composers of blues tunes. It was the "St. Louis Blues" and its success that won for Handy the title, "The Father of the Blues." Actually, Handy had earlier become famous for his "Memphis Blues," a tune that had started its career as a campaign song for the local mayorality race and which was turned into a popular song.

Writing about his "St. Louis Blues," William C. Handy has said: "'St. Louis Blues' was completed ... September, 1914. ... Two years had elapsed since I first published 'Memphis Blues.' ... Well, they say life begins at forty — I wouldn't know — but I was forty the year 'St. Louis Blues' was composed, and ever since then my life has, in one sense at least, revolved around that composition."[1]

The beginning of "St. Louis Blues" is almost too well known to need quoting:

Example 2

No detailed analysis can be given of a blues or jazz tune because, as has been previously stated, each performance is different: different breaks, different instruments in the performing ensemble, and so on. But regardless of the many variants that can occur, the tune itself is still the basis of "St. Louis Blues."

[1] William C. Handy, "Father of the Blues: An Autobiography" (New York: The Macmillan Company, 1941)

William C. Handy

(November 16, 1873-March 26, 1958)

William C. Handy was born in 1873 in a small town on the Tennessee River. Both of his parents had been slaves before the Civil War. Handy's father was a minister and did not approve of his son studying music at all! He once forced William to trade a guitar he had purchased with hard-earned money for a dictionary. Later William learned the trumpet from one of his teachers at school.

Handy became a fine trumpeter and toured with Mahara's Minstrels, and later formed a band of his own. Early in his career he was asked to write a piece of music for the election campaign of a man named Crump who was running for mayor of Memphis. The resulting composition, played for the first time on a bandwagon that was pulled by a team of horses through the streets of Memphis, was known as "Mr. Crump." The public liked it so well that Handy changed the piece's name to "Memphis Blues" and arranged to have it published. His career was thus launched.

MILES

by Miles Davis

Miles Davis is probably the most written about artist in the field of jazz. And he has many reputations: Miles the classy dresser; Miles the boxer; Miles the independent; Miles the pioneer. The word "pioneer" is appropriate, too, for over the past ten years Miles Davis has never stopped in his search for new sounds, new ways of performing music.

No matter where Miles Davis plays, his fans always pack the house. People come from all over to hear the one and only Miles Davis play his trumpet.

There is always a strong creative force at work within Davis, and each new record album of his proves that he has discovered still additional new directions. In music, Davis has incorporated the best of jazz, and the contemporary rock sounds and rhythms. His music has a flair for a long thematic line which reminds one of sixteenth-century composers. But

Davis' technique is of the twentieth century, for he uses polyrhythms (several rhythms at the same time), and polytonalities (different chords sounded simultaneously). He has come up with something new in jazz. The form is free, and from this freedom a wonderful group of compositions has sprung.

In his trumpet playing, Miles Davis has developed an unusual beauty of tone that gives warmth even to his most restrained, understated choruses. His playing has never lacked emotion, but the emotion has usually been contained, for he doesn't slap emotions at the listener. He is a "complete chorus" improvisor, taking the entire tune in stride. On either the open horn or with mute, be it trumpet or flugelhorn, his tone has vigor and strength. As you listen to the muted chorus in "Miles," for example, notice that the word "cool" no longer applies to it. The melody comes out with sureness, crystal-clear; one might even think of it as coming softly through deep velvet pile or pouring richly through silk fabric.

Miles Davis

(May 25, 1926-   )

Miles Dewey Davis III first became publically known for an unusual style of trumpet playing which he had developed, a style usually called the "cool school." Born in East St. Louis, Davis attended the Juilliard School of Music in New York City, then traveled to Los Angeles where he recorded with the famous Charlie Parker.

Davis next worked the 52nd Street clubs in New York before they became strip joints and then leveled. After his work with Parker, Davis started making some records of his own.

Many people cannot understand Davis as a person. On the band stand, neatly dressed, professionally poised and a complete master of his trumpet, Miles Davis seems to dare his audience to like him! He is unsmiling, unemotional, unshowmanly; many watching him work become bored because he looks bored. Many times Davis has simply turned his back to an audience as he plays his solo. But because of his beauty of tone, his musicianly accomplishments, he is a success.

Chapter X

MUSIC FOR THE STAGE

Music has been associated with stage productions for more than 2000 years. In ancient Greece, around 450 B.C., it was discovered that music — both instrumental and vocal — could heighten the dramatic effect of both comedies and tragedies. The dance also became part of their stage presentations.

During the Middle Ages (around the eleventh century) liturgical or religious plays became quite popular; once again music, through the use of songs and dances, was called upon to make the story more effective. "The Play of Daniel," which dates from a twelfth-century French manuscript, is an example; it is still performed in churches and theaters today. In it, an odd assortment of Medieval instruments accompany both the singing and dancing in a lavishly costumed presentation. The story and text are taken from the book of Daniel in the Bible.

In 1581 a ballet was performed at the French court in Versailles for a royal wedding. The dance was titled "Circe," named after the legendary Greek enchantress whose story the ballet portrayed. Appropriate costumes and stage scenery added to the spectacle. This was the beginning of ballet, in which dancing is combined with a dramatic plot. Although this early form used both vocal and instrumental music as well as spoken dialogue, the vocal music and spoken texts eventually disappeared . France became a leader in the field of classical ballet, and was followed in the nineteenth century by the Russian Imperial School of Ballet which reached its most glorious days when Tchaikovsky composed "Swan Lake" (1876), "The Sleeping Beauty" (1889) and "Nutcracker" (1892) for its productions. A new trend was started in the twentieth century when Serge Diaghilev, a ballet impressario from Russia who settled in Paris, encouraged such young musicians as Maurice Ravel to compose the ballet "Daphnes and Chloe" (1912) and Igor Stravinsky to write "Firebird" (1910), "Petrouchka" (1912) and "The Rite of Spring" (1913).

About the same time that ballet was coming into existence in France, a group of Italian noblemen were trying to re-create the music-dramas of classical Greece. These titled men in Florence, calling themselves the camerata — the "comrades" — produced the first of what they chose to call operas in 1597. Jacapo Peri provided music for the Greek legend of Dafne, using declamatory song accompanied by a few instruments, to convey the story with the additional aid of costumes and stage sets. This style of musical setting came to be known as <u>recitativo</u> (from "recitare", "to recite") in contrast to true songs and choruses in which, frequently, the text could not be understood completely in performance. Eventually opera incorporated all styles of writing; solo songs (known as <u>arias</u>), ensembles (duets, trios, quartets, etc.), recitatives, choruses, instrumental interludes and dances.

Opera spread from Italy to France and eventually to Germany. In France it became coupled with ballet in the works of Lully (b. 1632) and Rameau (b. 1683); for them the stage spectacle and the dance became the most important factors in opera. The Italians kept the vocal line supreme; the melodies of Rossini (b. 1792), Donizetti (b. 1797), Verdi (b. 1813) and Puccini (b. 1858) are well known today. In Germany, opera at first remained an Italian form and most German operas used Italian texts and were performed in Italian. Mozart's "Le Nozze de Figaro" (1786) — "The Marriage of Figaro" — is an example. Eventually they started using German texts. By the nineteenth century, the instrumental accompaniment became of major importance in German operas. In many of the works of Wagner (b. 1813) and Richard Strauss (b. 1864) the orchestra became so large and prominent that it frequently overpowered the vocal aspects of the music.

Throughout its history, opera made use of both comedies and tragedies for texts. Frequently in the comedies — known in Italian as <u>opera buffa</u> and in French as <u>opera comique</u> — part of the text was spoken so that the audience would have no difficulty in understanding the humorous lines and plot. The tragedies, using music throughout, sometimes used texts from the world's greatest playwrights. Verdi used Shakespeare's "Othello" and Debussy employed Maeterlinck's "Pelleas and Melisande" as texts. In other cases, mediocre plays were used; operas based on these have survived only if the music was superlative.

In the meantime, a new form was evolving in Paris and Vienna during the last half of the nineteenth century. It was a popular form modeled after opera and took for its name a diminutive form of that word, <u>operetta</u>. Using humorous stories and much spoken dialogue, the Frenchman Jacques Offenbach (b. 1819) and the Austrian Johann Strauss Jr. (b. 1825; no relation to Richard Strauss) created many memorable and frivolous stage works that were filled with melodious, popular tunes: "La Vie Parisienne" (1886) and "Die Fledermaus" (1874) are, respectively, among their best works. Both are still widely performed today.

The operetta style became very popular in the United States and led many Americans to try their hand at this type of composition. The most successful was Victor Herbert (b. 1859), whose "Naughty Marietta" (1910) and "Sweethearts" (1913) are still revived from time to time. Many composers followed this operetta trend, some calling their creations <u>light operas</u>. Suddenly, on April 1, 1943, a new type of work, <u>musical comedy</u> or <u>Broadway musical</u>, burst onto the scene when "Oklahoma!" was first produced at the St. James Theater in New York. Composer Richard Rodgers had teamed up with playwright Oscar Hammertsein II to create a work in which the songs and dances were a much more integral part of the story and drama. Rodgers and Hammerstein followed with many other memorable musicals: "Carousel," "South Pacific" and "The King and I."

Since some of the stories used, "Carousel" for example, were not truly comedies but actually, in several instances, tragedies, the name musical comedy was shortened to <u>musical</u>. Leonard Bernstein's musical, "West Side Story," would have to fall in this classification since its plot, a contemporary setting of Shakespeare's "Romeo and Juliet," is one of the greatest tragedies in all of literature.

DIE   MEISTERSINGER   VON   NÜRNBERG

by Richard Wagner

During the Middle Ages the nobility of central Europe established a leisurely way of life, free from wars and battles that had plagued their ancestors, a life given over to the enjoyment of lavish clothing, ornate furniture, enormous castles, rich food and much drink. Poet-musicians, writing poems of love, composing their own melodies and singing these songs for the lords and ladies of the manors. In southern France these artists were known as <u>troubadours,</u> in northern France they were called <u>trouveres.</u>

When these eleventh-century musicians traveled as far as Germany a century later, largely as a result of the Crusades, they made a great impression on the local people. Soon the German <u>minnesinger</u> (love-song singers) were attempting to do for the German nobility what the troubadours and trouveres had done for the French. By the thirteenth and fourteenth centuries, the German commoner — the peasants and craftsmen — wanted a share in this art of combining original poetry and music, so they formed guilds much as the cabinetmakers and tanners had earlier fromed their craft and trade guilds. The poet-musicians called their guild the <u>meistersinger,</u> the "mastersingers."

In the nineteenth century, more than 500 years later, the German operatic composer Richard Wagner became fascinated by the history of the meistersinger movement and decided to compose an opera whose setting would be placed in Medieval Germany during one of the song contests of this musical guild. For a central figure he chose an actual historical personage, one of the greatest of the early German poets, Hans Sachs. The composer chose to call this a "comic opera," although at first, it may seem that there isn't one good laugh in all the story. This is because the humor is more subtle. Through his story, Wagner attempted to show what fools would-be artists make of themselves when they attempt to create a work of art by rules and laws, lacking the least trace of artistic inspiration.

In Wagner's opera, which he called "Die Meistersinger von Nürnberg" ("The Mastersingers of Nuremberg"), a young knight by the name of Walter has fallen in love with Eva, the daughter of a rich goldsmith in Nuremberg. The old goldsmith, however, has promised his daughter's

hand in marriage to whomever wins the forthcoming song contest of the Mastersinger's Guild.

A stuffy and pompous fellow by the name of Beckmesser is also in love with Eva. Not only that, but he is to serve as a judge of the song contest. His job will be to tabulate any errors the contestants make in trying to follow the elaborate set of rules for the creation of a song which the Guild has established.

At the contest, Walter's "Trial Song" is unusual. Because of this, he makes a poor first impression on the Masters. Only the middle-age cobbler, Hans Sachs — himself a poet/musician of great ability — recognizes the originality and true beauty of Walter's song. Because Sachs also loves Eva, who is almost like a daughter to him, and because he desires her happiness, he helps Walter to win the contest and therefore Eva's hand in marriage.

In writing this opera, Wagner said that he had attempted to "contrast the spirit of folk-art with the narrow-minded, common mastersingers whose quite ridiculous laws and rules for writing poetry I suggested in the person of Beckmesser." He goes on to say that his story suggests the problems of "an artist like Walter who is faced by the stupid and angry criticism of the crowd."

Overture

Just as Wagner conceived his opera on several levels — that of the beauty of the music and love story, as well as that of a social satire on the hypocrisy of both the fourteenth and nineteenth centuries — so you can listen to the "Overture" on several levels. Separated as it will be in the classroom from the opera, it will probably be best to enjoy it purely as a piece of music. It can be enjoyed, however, also for its direct thematic relation to the story. The advanced pupil can even marvel at this "Overture" for the artistic and skillful manner in which it is musically constructed.

The "Overture" opens with the bold Meistersinger theme, the musical emblem of the guild of song writers. Played by the full orchestra, the twenty-seven measure Meistersinger theme begins:

Example 1

The second theme is introduced by a trill played by woodwinds and strings. This melody, which in the opera suggests Walter's love for Eva, is played first by the flute.

Example 2

A rapid and brilliant scale passage introduces the next theme, a Meistersinger fanfare. This melody was adapted by Wagner from an actual tune of the real fourteenth-century Meistersin ger. It is played by the winds; the strings accompany with ascending runs. The strings then join the winds to complete the statement of the theme.

Example 3

A superb expansion of a theme heard in the final chorus of the opera, as Hans Sachs delivers his speech in praise of German art, follows:

114

Example 4

The melody of Walter's "Prize Song" is now heard:

Example 5

Six measures later, this theme, Example 5, is interrupted by a short, impatient melody in the violins, whose tune comes from a song which Walter sings in the first act of the opera. This section is marked by several changes of tonality.

Example 6

With a stroke of genius, Wagner now depicts the tottering apprentices of the guild, those doddering men who know the rules so well but who lack a single spark of talent among them, by using the majestic "Meister-singer theme, Example 1. However, to suggest the busy-bodies that the apprentices really are, the composer cuts the time values of the tones of the theme by a third, known to the musician as <u>diminution</u>, making it sound anything but noble and majestic.

Example 7

After several measures of woodwind trills and a rapid succession of sixteenth-notes played by the violins, Wagner, in a magnificent piece of writing, combines three of the major themes. The trumpets and horns start off with the fanfare theme, Example 3; the violins play Walter's "Prize Song" melody, Example 5; and the basses and lower winds take up the majestic Meistersinger theme, Example 1.

Example 8

After a dynamic climax, the fanfare theme, Example 3, is boldly restated.

The "Overture" concludes with the opening Meistersinger theme, Example 1, in a final, dramatic presentation.

Diminution: When a theme or melody is repeated with notes of lesser time value, the melody is said to be repeated in diminution.

Diacritical Marks: The composer, to better inform the performer of his intent, frequently uses symbols and words to indicate how a note or a passage should be performed. In most music, these words are in Italian (the so-called "language of music"), but starting in the late nineteenth century, composers other than those of Italian origin started using their native language to convey their meanings in addition to the traditional Italian expressions. Examples of this are:

sehr gehalten (German)	very sustained
ausdrucksvoll (German)	expressive
aber ausdrucksvoll (German)	again expressive
immer (German) ff (Italian)	always very loud (fortissimo)
sehr zart (German)	very tenderly
dolce (Italian)	sweetly
sehr markert (German)	very marked

Richard Wagner

(May 22, 1813 - February 13, 1883)

Richard Wagner led a troubled and turbulent life. Early in his youth he became convinced that he was a genius; he started writing his autobiography at sixteen so that the world would have a record of the life and activities of this genius!

Political revolutions were going on in Germany when Wagner was a young man first establishing himself as a composer. Unfortunately he aligned himself with the losing side, and so fled from Germany to Paris as a political exile. Since he was convinced that he was a musical genius, he decided that the world owed him a luxurious life. Without worrying about the source of money to pay for things, he ran up staggering bills in Paris. The French finally threw him into debtor's prison.

Eventually he was able to gain release from prison; he returned to his native land. One day a young monarch, King Ludwig II, sent for Wagner. He was so fascinated with the composer's music that he not only offered to pay off all of Wagner's debts and give him a large income on which to live, he also wanted to provide enough money to build a special opera house to be designed by Wagner. Only Wagner's operas were to be given in the Bayreuth Festspielhaus once it was completed.

Wagner is remembered chiefly as an operatic composer. His most famous operas include "Lohengrin," "Tannhauser," the "Ring of the Nibelungen" (a series of four operas), "Tristan and Isolde" (one of the world's greatest love stories), and "Parsifal" (his "sacred" opera, based on the legend of the Holy Grail).

S W A N   L A K E

by Peter Ilyitch Tchaikovsky

The Tchaikovsky family gathered during the summer of 1869 at Kamenka, a resort in the Ukrain district of Russia. The composer, still a bachelor at 29, joined them after completing work on his second opera. He entered into the holiday spirit of **family fun**, joining in the games of his nieces and nephews: building bonfires in the woods on balmy evenings, playing follow-the-leader in jumping ditches and running about, and other spirited activities of youngsters.

Although outwardly a quiet man, given over to the deepest despair at times, Tchaikovsky loved his family. For the amusement of his nieces he wrote that summer some ballet music to which they could dance. It was the first brief form of "Swan Lake," based on an ancient fairy tale.

He forgot about the music until a commission arrived six years later from the Director of the Moscow Opera, a request to compose a full-length ballet. Tchaikovsky had never tried professionally to write a ballet before. The examples of ballet music that were then in current use in the opera houses were works written by third- and fourth-rate composers, music devised — not artistically — simply to provide a background for the excellent Corps de Ballet, the dance company. At first Tchaikovsky was despondent, full of self-doubt. He wrote to his sister:

> "There are hours, days, weeks — yes, even months — when everything looks black and I am tormented by the thought that I am forsaken and no one loves me. And why should they? What use am I to anyone? If I vanished from this earth today it would be no great loss to Russian music and no great loss to anyone personally."

Fortunately his sister invited him to stay with her family in the Ukrain that summer. His spirits rose, and he quickly finished writing his third symphony and turned to the music for the commissioned ballet. He returned to the fairy tale of "Swan Lake," and, making use of some of the themes that he had written many summers earlier, he completed the Prologue and first act of the ballet within two weeks.

Other tasks then occupied his attention and he didn't return to "Swan Lake" until the following Easter when he again spent another holiday in the country. This time he completed the score. The first performance was scheduled for the Bolshoi Theater with the Imperial Ballet Company. The production was a complete disaster! Everything that could go wrong, did. The costumes didn't fit the dancers, the stage sets were a disgrace. The choreography was poorly designed, the dancers were among the worst of the Corps and the orchestra did not rehearse the music. The Director hacked out whole sections of Tchaikovsky's music and substituted trite pieces by other composers. "Swan Lake" fell into disfavor and was not performed again in Tchaikovsky's lifetime. Twenty years after its premiere performance, a new version was worked out by Marius Petipa, a choreographer; the new production swept the world. Since then, "Swan Lake" has been one of the world's favorite ballets.

The story is a simple one. A sorcerer by the name of Rothbart has changed the beautiful princess Odette, along with her friends, into swans. Only at night can they assume their original human forms. A handsome young prince, Siegfried, discovers Odette in human form one evening beside the lake. It is love at first sight!

Odette, however, tells Siegfried of the fate that has befallen her. She tells him that the evil magician's spell can be broken only if Siegfried remains faithful to her and never woos another. At the ball the next evening, Siegfried successfully ignores all the beautiful young women who flirt with him until a dark and beautiful girl appears on the arm of a strange knight. The knight is the evil Rothbart, and the girl is his daughter Odile, whom he has transformed into the very image of Odette. (The same ballerina usually dances both roles, dressed in white as Odette, in black as Odile.) Unfortunately, Siegfried declares his love for this girl whom he thinks is Odette. Rothbart reveals the deception, and with a laugh of triumph, disappears with Odile.

Siegfried returns to the lake and his beloved white swan. Odette forgives him since he had been deceived. Now that she is condemned forever on earth to be a swan, she and Siegfried decide they would prefer death so that they can be reunited in the next world. They then cast themselves into the lake.

Waltz

During the second act of "Swan Lake," a ball is given by Siegfried's mother to honor his twenty-first birthday. It is at this dance that Siegfried at first ignores all the beautiful young girls. A brilliant waltz serves as a prelude to this scene.

The "Waltz" is sectional in nature; two interludes separate the repetitions of its principal melody.

Melodically, an inverted arch opens the "Waltz." The strings, pizzicato, play a long, descending scale; the direction then turns and they play an ascending arpeggio which ends in three loud chords.

The low strings and horn establish the oom-pah-pah rhythm of a waltz. The violins, now bowed, softly play the principal theme of the "Waltz," Example 1. They repeat it an octave higher in pitch, this time descending figures in the upper woodwinds accompany it.

Example 1

violins

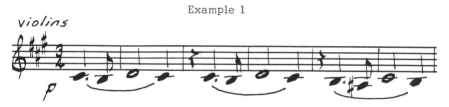

Suddenly the strings take up a bold theme, fortissimo: Example 2. It, too, is repeated.

Example 2

violins

The first interlude opens softly; the eight-measure melody is accompanied by sustained chords. It is repeated.

Example 3

Example 3 is repeated _mf_ against an accompanying passage in eighth-notes for the strings. In turn, this is repeated.

In the next eight-measure passage, also repeated, the woodwinds take over the eighth-note figures while the strings suggest Example 3.

The woodwinds continue their figures as the dynamic level drops; the strings now play pizzicato.

Suddenly, in a passage marked fortissimo, the melody of Example 3 returns. Its repetition marks the end of the first interlude.

The principal theme, Example 1, returns; the violins play it first in the lower octave, then repeat it in the higher octave. The bold second theme, Example 2, follows as it did the first time, and is repeated.

The second interlude opens with a melody started softly by the violins and completed by the winds, Example 4. Example 4 is repeated.

Example 4

A trumpet tune is heard next, Example 5. The trumpet repeats the tune.

Example 5

The melody of Example 4 is heard once again, softly.
The violins take up Example 6, softly. It is repeated three times.

Example 6

The violins turn to a new melody, Example 7, which grows in dynamic intensity. Example 7 is repeated.

Example 7

Example 6 returns in the violins. After its repetition, a long crescendo starts as the strings and winds climb ever higher in pitch. At the climax of this passage, a variant of Example 3 from the first interlude is played by the full orchestra. Fragments of it are repeated on successively higher pitches.

At the major dynamic climax of the waltz, while strings, woodwinds and upper brasses are playing fortissimo, the trombones return to a variant of the principal theme, Example 1, leading to the brilliant conclusion of the "Waltz."

Peter Ilyitch Tchaikovsky

(May 7, 1840 – November 6, 1893)

Peter Tchaikovsky was born in a little mining town in the Ural mountains of Russia; his father was a mining engineer. Peter was the second child of a family of five boys (two of them twins) and one girl.

He received a good education; a French governess supervised his training. Although he started piano lessons when he was four and had tried his hand at composition by the time he was ten, neither he nor his family attached any significance to music or suspected his ability in the field was anything other than average. After completing his basic studies, he was sent iff to law school in St. Petersburg (now Leningrad). His still casual interest in music led him to continue music lessons while he was at law school. Upon graduation, Tchaikovsky found a position as a minor clerk in the Ministry of Justice.

When a new Conservatory of Music opened, he signed up for some studies at its evening sessions. He had already come to the conclusion that sooner or later "I shall exchange civil service in the Ministry for music. Don't imagine that I dream of becoming a great artist. I only want to do the work for which I feel I have some ability. Whether I become a celebrated composer or a poor music teacher — it's all the same."

In less than six months Tchaikovsky resigned from the Ministry and concentrated on music. It was a risky step to take since his father's financial condition was so poor that he could only provide a very small allowance for his son's room and board. Peter found it necessary to give music lessons to increase his financial position, while he studied full time at the Conservatory.

After graduation, Tchaikovsky joined the staff of the Conservatory in Moscow and started to work on his first symphony. He stayed awake nights worrying about it. He bordered on a nervous breakdown over its completion. He almost gave up composition as being too strenuous for his nerves. This was to be the pattern of his life; he frequently worried in later years, after being very successful, that his source of inspiration had dried up. Nevertheless, Tchaikovsky composed some of the most popular music in the concert repertory.

The composer in 1880

Chapter XI
MUSIC FOR THE VOICE

Music for the solo voice evolved in all civilizations long before any form of instrumental music since no one had to discover how to make or build an instrument or learn a technique of playing it. Primitive vocal music served three purposes: it provided a means of communication, it served as entertainment through the use of secular songs, and it heightened the effect of worship services through sacred songs. Some music evolved over a long period of time through the efforts of many unknown, musically untrained people. This we call folk music. Other compositions were the result of the skillful technique and artistry of a single person. Not until after 1400 was such a person's name actually attached to the music as its composer.

During the Baroque era, roughly from the birth of opera in 1600 to about 1750, both sacred and secular vocal music began to be associated with dramatic stage presentations. The birth of opera was described in the previous chapter, "Music for the Stage"; closely paralleling the development of the operatic form was the evolution of the oratorio. At first there was little technical difference between the two, although operas were usually based on secular stories and seemed to call for more dramatic action on stage as opposed to the oratorio's more static nature, whether secular or sacred. Oratorios usually involved more pageantry and history than operatic productions, which for their texts leaned more to interesting myths and legends. Oratorios, like opera, at first were fully staged with sets and costumes, and were scored for soloists, choruses and orchestra. The development of this form reached its zenith in the more than twenty oratorios by Georg Friederich Handel, many of them sacred.

To distinguish a composed song from a folk song, the term art song has been widely used. The composers of the Classical era, roughly from 1750 to 1830, wrote many art songs, men such as Haydn, Mozart and Beethoven. The development of excellent poetry during the Romantic era, in the nineteenth century, inspired composers to set some of it to music. Nobody before or since has surpassed the songs written by Franz Schubert. The fusion of text and vocal line, all integrated with an artistic piano accompaniment, led to a very special category of art song to which the German word lied, meaning "song," is generally applied, Other outstanding composers of lieder (the plural of "lied") during the Roman-

123

tic era include Robert Schumann, Johannes Brahms and Hugo Wolf.

In modern times, composers have explored all the possibilities of tonal color or timbre. This naturally led to the investigation of effects that could be derived from using the human voice in combinations with instruments. Debussy used a wordless chorus of women's voices in his orchestral composition "Sirens" to suggest those water-nymphs who, according to mythology, lured sailors to their lair. Puccini suggested the calm serenity of evening by closing Act II of his opera "Madama Butterfly" by scoring the melody for a chorus of women's voices humming the melody in unison. In contrast, Schoenberg tried to effect a cross between singing and speaking in a technique which he called sprechstimme, "speech-song," in his chamber work "Pierrot Lunaire."

By the early 1970s, lieder recitals in concert halls were on the decline, while there was a tremendous surge of popular interest in folk songs which had started in the late 1960s. Opera, largely a European form, thrived there while it made only moderate progress in the United States. The oratorio form, largely unused by composers since the Baroque era, had limited appeal and was represented chiefly by one work, Handel's "Messiah," a sacred oratorio performed in many churches around Christmas each year. Hybrid works such as Leonard Bernstein's "Mass: A Theater Piece for Singers, Players and Dancers" contrasted traditional liturgical texts and an oratorio style with contemporary poetry and rock.

BACHIANAS BRASILEIRAS NO. 5

by Heitor Villa-Lobos

The modern Brazilian composer, Heitor Villa-Lobos, led a very unusual life, one greatly different from that of most symphonic composers. As a youth, he hated school and formal education. Therefore, in music, he was largely self-taught. From his earliest days he was fascinated by the folk music and popular music of his native Rio de Janeiro. It was only logical, then, that when he started composing, his first works were popular songs. Later, when he turned to symphonic compositions, his writing was greatly influenced by both Brazilian folk melodies and native folk instruments. His music, thus, was always Brazilian in flavor, always different than that of the traditional European composers.

To serve his purpose, he devised two categories of compositions which he called "choros" and "Bachianas Brasileiras." The choros, of which he wrote fourteen, represented street serenades which emphasized the rhythm and popular melodies of Brazilian, Indian and popular music. The Bachianas Brasileiras are a combination of contrapuntal writing, based on the earlier style of Johann Sebastian Bach, and native elements of Brazilian music. He composed nine of these latter suites.

Asked about the Bachianas Brasileiras, the composer said that they were "a special kind of musical composition based on a knowledge of the great works of J. S. Bach, and also based on my love of the harmony and melody of the folk music of the north-east region of Brazil." He went on to say that he composed "in folk style. ... An artist must do this. He must select and transmit the material given him by his people. ... I study the history, the country, the speech, the customs, the background of the people. I have always done this, and it is from these sources, spiritual as well as practical, that I have drawn my art."

Each of the Bachianas Brasileiras suites is scored for a different instrumental combination, much the same way in which each of the suites of Bach is scored for varying groups of instruments. The "Bachianas Brasileiras No. 5" is scored for eight solo cellos and a soprano soloist. There are two movements in the suite. The first is titled "Aria" and was completed in 1938. The second movement, "Dansa" (or "dance") was added in 1945.

Aria

Two of the eight cellos double the soprano melody in the "Aria;" the other cellos provide the accompaniment which is predominantly pizzicato, suggesting the native guitars of Brazil. In the first and last sections of this movement in ternary form, the soprano sings without words on a neutral syllable. In the middle section the words are from a poem by Ruth V. Corrêa in Portuguese.

The "Aria" opens with a two-measure introduction. In the contrapuntal style of Bach, the upper and lower instrumental voices move in contrary (opposite) motion.

The soprano enters on the neutral syllable "ah." The melody, the beginning of which is quoted in Example 1, is long phrased, lyric, and employs melodic turns characteristic of native Brazilian music. While this melody is not a folk theme, it suggests folk music. Although the meter changes frequently, the pulsations (beats) are steady and equal; the onward "push" of this rhythm is a Brazilian characteristic.

Example 1*

Four measures after the excerpt quoted in Example 1, the melodic line is built out of a series of sequences — repeated figures on differing pitch levels.

* "Bachianas Brasileiras No. 5" by Heitor Villa-Lobos copyright 1947 by Associated Music Publishers, Inc. Used by permission.

Example 2

Following the statement of this melody, a three measure interlude occurs.

The melody, starting with Example 1, is then repeated by a solo cello; the voice is silent during this repetition.

The middle section resembles a popular Brazilian tune. It is full of syncopation and rubatos — misplaced accents and slight accelerations or retards in the tempo. The soloist sounds almost as if she were improvising or creating the melody as she sings along. The harmony is particularly interesting. It begins:

Example 3

Tarde, una nuvein rosea	Lo at midnight clouds are slowly
Lenta e transparente,	Passing, rosy and lustrous,
Sobre o espaço sonhadora	O'er the spacious heav'n with
e bella!	loveliness laden!
Surge no infinito a lua	From the boundless deep the
docemente,	moon arises wondrous
Enfeitando a tarde	Glorifying the evening
Qual meiga donzela	Like a beauteous maiden,
Que se apresta	Now she adorns herself
E alinda sonhadoramente,	In half unconscious duty,
Em anseios d'alma	Eager, anxious
Para ficer bella,	That we recognize her beauty,
Grita so céo e a terra,	While sky and earth, yea,
Toda a Natureza!	All nature salutes her!
Cala a passarada aos seus	All the birds have ceased their
tristes queixumes,	sad and mournful complaining,

E reflete o mar toda a
   sua riqueza
Suave a luz da lua desperta
   agora,
A cruel saudade que rie chora!
	Now appears on the sea in a
	   silver reflection
	Moonlight softly waking the
	   soul and constraining
	Hearts to cruel tears and
	   bitter dejection!

Tarde una nuvein rosea
Lenta e transparente,
Sobre o espaco sonhadora
   e bella!
	Lo at midnight clouds are slowly
	Passing, rosy and lustrous,
	O'er the spacious heav'n with
	   loveliness laden!

The voice returns to the original melody, starting with Example 1. This time the soprano hums with closed mouth, a very difficult feat.

Heitor Villa-Lobos

(March 5, 1887 – November 17, 1959)

Born in Rio de Janeiro, Villa-Lobos received his first musical instruction at six from his father who was an amateur cellist and pianist. Heitor taught himself the violin, learning to play it by holding the instrument in a vertial position such as one does a cello! A brief encounter with formal musical training followed: first, studies at the Conservatory; then, later, a private teacher for composition. Heitor hated the classroom, disliked formal studies. He gave up.

Villa-Lobos was eleven when his father died; he then stopped going to school altogether. He turned to playing popular music in theater and restaurant orchestras. Every free moment he spent in various haunts which specialized in the popular songs and dances of Brazil. He composed a number of popular songs himself. He tried to complete his musical training at the National Institute of Music in Rio de Janeiro, but soon gave that up, too. His first symphonic composition, "Canticos Sertanejos," a suite for orchestra based on Brazilian country airs, was completed in 1909, when Villa-Lobos was twenty-two.

In 1912, Villa-Lobos made the first of many trips to the interior of Brazil to discover more about the music, rites and ceremonies of the natives who lived there. He was now inspired to compose one work after another. By 1915, a concert devoted exclusively to his works was given in Rio de Janeiro. Unfortunately the public wasn't ready for his style of composition. For the average symphony patron — oriented in the European tradition — the music of Villa-Lobos smacked of Brazilian popular music and folk rhythms; for the man-in-the-street who enjoyed popular music, Villa-Lobos' compositions were too formal!

Villa-Lobos lived in Paris, on and off, from 1923 to 1930, then returned to Brazil to become its Director of Musical Education. In 1944 Villa-Lobos visited the United States for the first time and was commissioned by the Boston Symphony Orchestra to write a work for their "Villa-Lobos Week." For the next fifteen years, Villa-Lobos divided his time between New York and Rio de Janeiro. Of his more than 1500 compositions, he is best remembered for his nine Bachianas Brasileiras and twelve choros (both described earlier in detail), eleven symphonies, some songs, chamber music and film scores.

LIEBESLIEDER WALZER

Opus 52

by Johannes Brahms

Although Brahms is known to the concert-going public primarily as an orchestral composer, much of his early training, experience and compositional efforts centered around vocal music. When he was in his teens, one of his first professional positions was a summer job obtained near his home city of Hamburg, Germany, conducting a male chorus. For them he made numerous musical settings of folk songs.

At twenty-four he served the small German town of Lippe-Detmold as a conductor of their choral society, and, during the summer, directed the Women's Choir of Hamburg. Many of Brahms' shorter choral works were composed for the Women's Choir. After three years of this association, he moved to Vienna where he accepted a position as conductor of the Singakademie. Several of his major choral works were written after this appointment, including the "German Requiem."

In the spring of 1869 Brahms went to Karlsruhe to conduct a performance of this "German Requiem." He rented an apartment there, and during the first six weeks of his stay he was truly inspired. He was happy, carefree and felt encouraged by the public's enthusiastic acceptance of his works. By early July he had completed twenty of the waltzes of the "Liebeslieder Walzer" ("The Love-Song Waltzes").

Brahms selected eighteen of these waltzes to be published in his first set (Opus 52). The poems he set were from the folk poetry of Russia and Poland. They had been translated into German by Georg Friedrich Daumer and published as a collection under the title, "Polydora." Brahms' original setting of these selected poems was for four solo voices — soprano, contralto, tenor and bass — and two pianos. Brahms later arranged them for a piano duet and some for voices with small orchestra. The first performance of the original took place in Karlsruhe in October. Clara Schumann, the widow of composer Robert Schumann and Brahms' closest friend, was one of the pianists; the conductor Hermann Levi was the other.

Ein kleiner, hübscher Vogelnahm (No. 6)

The sixth waltz, "Ein kleiner, hübscher Vogelnahm" ("There Was a Tiny, Little Bird"), is a light and gracious waltz that speaks of love that flits about as if it were a bird — sometimes hard to catch, always flighty.

Three pair of repeated notes serve as an introduction to Number 6 which is marked "Grazioso" (graceful). The tenor soloist introduces the first melody:

Example 1

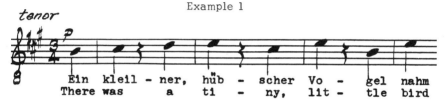

The other three voices respond; the soprano melody is a melodic and rhythmic variant of Example 1.

Wenn ich ein hübscher, kleiner
   Vogel wür',
Ich säumte nicht, ich täte so
   wieder.

If I were a tiny, little bird so
   fair,
I'd fly away and seek a garden
   lair.

A tenor-bass duet follows; they are answered by a soprano-contralto duet. The tenor starts:

Example 2

All four voices now take up the melody of Example 2; the text is the same. The passage ends with various statements of "nicht fort" — "no more, no more."

The first piano takes up the melody of Example 1 while the tenor soloist sings a counter-melody, Example 3.

Example 3

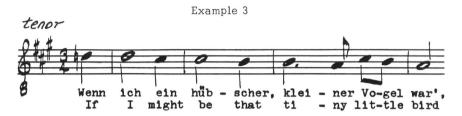

| Wenn | ich | ein | hüb | - scher, | klei | - ner | Vo-gel | war', |
| If | I | might | be | that | ti | - ny | lit-tle | bird |

The other three soloists answer with their melodic variant of Example 1.
A lyrical section in F major follows. The tenor soloist starts off and is soon joined by the other three soloists. The passage, Example 4, is repeated.

Example 4

| Der__ | Vo - | gel__ | kam, | Der__ | Vo - | gel__ | kam, |
| That__ | bird | did__ | light, | That__ | bird | did__ | light |

After a brief piano interlude, a melodic variant of Example 4 is heard. The text for this section, which is, in its turn repeated, is:

Da tat es ihm,   And there he had
Dem Glücklichen, nicht and.   A fair, delightful stand.

The music modulates (changes tonality) back to A major. The tenor soloist repeats his original melody, Example 1, to the same text. Once more the other three voices respond. A few statements of "wie der" — "I'd fly" — follow, and the waltz is over.

> Modulation: When the tonality (key) of a composition changes through a chord or series of chords, a modulation takes place. The modulation is usually accomplished by passing through a chord that is common to both the old and new tonalities. The common chord is called a "pivotal" chord. To be a true modulation, a perfect cadence (a dominant followed by a tonic chord of the new tonality) must follow.

Johannes Brahms

(May 7, 1833 – April 3, 1897)

For a biographical sketch of Johannes Brahms, see page 100.

THE TROUT

by Franz Schubert

For Franz Schubert, writing a song was as natural a thing to do as eating or taking long strolls around his home in Vienna. He was fourteen when he composed his first song, seventeen when he wrote one of his finest, "Margaret at the Spinning Wheel." His most popular song, "The Erl King," was completed when Schubert was eighteen. In all, he composed more than 550 songs, an average of more than thirty songs a year.

In 1817, Schubert was then twenty, the composer took a year's leave of absence from his classroom teaching position in his father's school. He decided against living at home and took up lodging with a friend of his. He hoped to pay for his room and board by money earned from the sale of his compositions, by taking music pupils, and by writing for the theater. The future looked bright!

In this happy environment, the composer quickly dashed off some piano sonatas, some overtures, some chamber music. Although these instrumental compositions occupied most of his interest, he still managed to create fifty songs in the year 1817. Two of them were outstanding: "The Trout" and "Death and the Maiden."

Although Schubert had composed many songs to texts by the best German poets — Goethe for example — he was happy setting any poem that was conveniently at hand. A close friend, Christian Schubart, gave young Franz a poem he had just finished; its story told of a trout's valiant fight against the craftiness of a fisherman.

Schubert sat down at the keyboard and commenced to work. As was his habit, he would not leave the piano until the song was finished. It was past midnight before he notated the final chord on paper. "In my haste," he said, "I then rather sleepily picked up the ink well instead of the bottle of blotting sand, and poured ink quite calmly over my manuscript. What a disaster!"

The song was an instant success with Schubert's friends and he had soon dashed off half-a-dozen more copies for them. (It is strange to note that the original ink-blotted copy was reproduced in facsimile in 1870, and then, incredibly, lost!)

The original copy did not include a piano introduction to the song; this was added in a later one. In the introduction, the piano suggests the rippling of the brook:

Example 1

The manuscript of *The Trout*, with the famous blot

Against a continuation of this type of accompaniment, the voice introduces the simple but beautiful melody of "The Trout":

Example 2

In ei-nem Bäch-lein hel-le, da schoss in fro-her Eil'
In yon-der flow-ing brooklet, Ap-pear'd a playful trout

A contrasting phrase follows:

Example 3

Ich stand an dem Ge - sta- de und sah in sü - sser Ruh
On schore I stood with pleasure, Content to stand and look

A four-measure piano interlude separates the next stanza which is musically identical to the first. Its text:

Ein Fischer mit der Ruthe
Wohl an dem Ufer stand,
Und sah's mit kaltem Blute,
Wie sich das Fischlein wand.

With pole and fish line waiting
An angler came that way,
And saw with great enjoyment
The trout below him play.

So lang' dem Wasser Helle,
So dacht' ich, nicht gebricht,
So fängt er die Forelle
Mit seiner Angel nicht.

I thought if clear the water
Continues round about
The man would never capture
My silver little trout.

The music now changes to the minor mode; the thought — both musically and poetically — becomes sinister.

Example 4

Doch end-lich ward dem Die - be die Zeit zu lang,
At last the craft-y ang - ler, As time went by,

A return to the major mode occurs; the final lines of the text are set to melodic variants of fragments from Example 3:

Example 5

und ich mit re - gem Blu - te sah die Be -trog'ne an,
And tak-en from the brooklet,Quite needlessly I thought

The five measure postlude is the same as the five measure introduction.

Art Song: In contrast to folk songs which evolve over a period of time and are the creation of many unknown, musically untrained people, art songs are vocal solos created by a single, named composer of serious music.

Lied (plural: lieder) : The art songs composed by Franz Schubert and his Germanic followers — Robert Schumann, Johannes Brahms, Hugo Wolf and others — are called lieder. They are settings of especially fine poems in which the vocal line and piano accompaniment share in the artistic interest of the composition.

Franz Schubert

(January 31, 1797 - November 19, 1828)

The life of Franz Schubert was short, a bare thirty-one years. During those brief years he achieved little fame; he never appeared in public as a soloist or conductor. He almost never took a composer's bow after one of his new works was publicly performed. Most of his 550 songs, eight or nine symphonies, fifteen stage works, piano and chamber music were unknown to the public at the time of his death.

He was born in a suburb of Vienna, the twelfth of the fourteen children of school teacher Franz Schubert and his wife. The elder Franz Schubert planned that his namesake should also become a school teacher. He started him on the violin when he was eight and saw to it that the boy's older brother Ignaz gave him piano lessons. The church organist provided lessons in singing, organ playing and theory for the boy.

At eleven, Franz was enrolled in the Imperial Royal Chapel Choir School, called curiously in Austrian the "Konvict." The school was conducted in a drab-looking building that did, indeed, look like a prison. In exchange for young Franz' services as a singer in the choir — the "Vienna Choirboys" — he received free room and board, musical instruction and a general education. During his five years at the school he played violin in their orchestra which gave a concert every night. His first song was composed at fourteen, and several overtures, many more songs, a string quartet, and his first symphony — written for the school's orchestra — were composed while he was a student.

After leaving the Konvict, he was enrolled for a time in St. Anne's School where he was trained to be a school teacher. At seventeen he became an assistant teacher to his father. Unenthusiastic about the job, he did more composing at his desk than he did teaching of the A - B - C's. Within two years he had composed two of his finest songs, "Margaret at the Spinning Wheel" and "The Erl King" in addition to four symphonies.

Friends encouraged Schubert to leave his teaching post and devote his time to composition. From this date onward, the composer never had a steady income or permanent place of residence. He lived first with one friend and then another. He continued to compose great quantities of music. For the few that were published in his lifetime, he was paid about 20¢ apiece!

Chapter XII

MUSIC FOR STRINGS

The orchestral stringed instruments which we know today — the violin, the viola, the violoncello (to give the cello its full name) and the string bass or bass viol — have evolved over a long period of time. They were not "invented" on any certain date or by any one person.

The violin, the principal member of the string family, probably emerged about 1550, if by violin we mean a four stringed instrument, played on the arm by a bow, without frets (metal strips fitted to the fingerboard of instruments such as the banjo and guitar to facilitate the stopping of a string), and tuned in fifths upward from "g". The early violin combined features of several still earlier instruments: the rebec, the Renaissance fiddle and the lira da braccio.

The greatest strides in violin-making took place during the middle of the sixteenth century in northern Italy, mainly in the towns of Brescia and Cremona. A century later, Cremona produced the greatest violin-maker of them all, Antonio Stradivari (1644-1737). His teacher, Niccolò Amati (1596-1684) made some outstanding violins still in use today, while another craftsman of the Cremona group, Giuseppe Guarneri del Gesù (1698-1744) also contributed some of today's finest violins.

About 1800 the violin underwent its last important change. Up to this time most music had been performed by small groups in the private chambers of kings and nobility; with the French revolution and other political and social changes throughout Europe, the performance of music moved to large public concert halls with the general citizenry paying admission fees to hear the concerts. Larger halls meant the need for a greater volume of sound. To this end, several minor modifications were made in the violin: the playing pitch was raised, the bridge was heightened, the length of the string was increased by a quarter of an inch to a half inch. These factors meant that several parts of the violin were altered: the angle of the fingerboard, the length of the fingerboard, the size of the bridge.

The bow with which the violin is played has changed considerably over the years. Originally it was convex, shaped like a hunter's bow from which it probably took its name. These early bows were made of snakewood and horsehair, the playing length of the hair varying from eighteen to twenty-three inches. The hair was made taut by hooking the thumb around the hair at the end of the bow to achieve the necessary ten-

sion. The further development of the bow was centered chiefly in the areas of straightening the bow and devising ways of regulating the tension of the hair.

François Tourte (1747-1835), a Frenchman, had much to do with standardizing the modern form of the bow. As a bow-maker, he chose Pernambuco wood (a species of Brazilwood) so that his bows had greater weight, strength and elasticity. He established twenty-nine and a quarter inches as the overall length of the bow, twenty-five and a half inches as the playing length of the hair. He devised an adjustable nut for the end of the bow which could regulate the tension of the horsehair.

The modern violin, simple as it looks to the eye, is really a complicated assemblage of over seventy parts. Essentially the instrument is a hollow box, usually fourteen inches long. Its four strings are stretched over a bridge made of maple. The top of the instrument, sometimes called the "table" or "belly," is made of soft wood, usually European spruce, while the back is made of hard wood, generally maple. Both back and top are arched. The neck, head, scroll and ribs (which join top and back) are also usually made of maple. The fingerboard, nut, saddle and tailpiece are of ebony; the pegs may be either ebony or rosewood. Modern chin rests are made of either wood or plastic.

Inside the violin there are top, bottom and corner blocks as well as the side linings to give added strength. Also inside are the soundpost and bass bar which serve as supports. The soundpost is usually made of spruce and is located behind the right foot of the bridge. The soundholes (sometimes called the "f holes" because of their shape) and the bridge serve an important acoustical function. Varnish is used on the finished instrument as a preservative. While the varnish cannot improve the tone, it can affect it.

Originally the violin was held against the upper chest in performance, much in the manner of some contemporary fiddle-players in Country and Western bands. Leopold Mozart (1719-1787), the composer's father, suggested in his book on violin technique that holding the violin under the chin gave the performer a much firmer grip on the instrument and permitted the right hand to move quickly up and down the fingerboard without having to help support the instrument. Soon this method of holding the violin was widely accepted.

The viola is the alto member of the string family and is tuned a fifth lower than the violin. It is not certain whether the modern viola preceded or succeeded the development of the violin; for all intents and purposes, they were simultaneous. The development of its bow paralleled that of the violin bow.

The construction of the viola, as well as its outward appearance, is identical to that of the violin except that it is one-seventh larger in size, measuring about sixteen and a quarter to sixteen and three quarter inches in length.

The violoncello is the tenor member of the string family. Although it looks identical to the viola (except that it is twice the size), there are several important differences. The proportions of length and breadth are about the same, but the depth is increased in order to provide an enclosed area big enough to give the necessary resonance to the lower tones.

The cello (to use the common abbreviated form of the name) evolved about the same time as the violin and viola, one of the earliest being made by Andrea Amati in Cremona about 1572.

The bass member of the string family goes by several different names although they all refer to the same instrument. It is sometimes called the bass viol or the double bass; both these names come from the full name, double bass viol. Occasionally it is referred to as the contrabass, the English form of the French contrabasse or German Kontrabass or Italian contrabasso.

This instrument differs in its external appearance from the other stringed instruments, for the slope of its upper shoulders is both different and narrower. This is because the instrument is derived from the old viol family which preceeded the violin family (although the two families are only slightly related).

The double bass dates from the sixteenth century and has never achieved the "standardization" that the other stringed instruments have known. The average bass stands over six feet high with a forty-four inch body. It usually has four strings, but sometimes there is an extension on one string or a fifth string so that the instrument can play down to the "c" an octave below the lowest tone of the cello. Sometimes the instrument has an arched back, but most have a flat back to make it easier to hold and play. The bass is tuned in fourths, not fifths, since the distance between two adjacent tones is about as far as the fingers of the human hand can comfortably stretch on a string some forty-two inches long.

There are two principal types of bows in use today for the double bass. The French bow resembles the cello bow although it is thicker, heavier and more sharply curved. It is held in the same approximate position as the cello bow. The German bow has a greater curve and is held like a meat-saw, allowing greater pressure to be put upon the strings.

The earliest orchestras — groups of instruments of more than chamber size such as trios, quartets and quintets — were comprised exclusively of stringed instruments. Most of the stringed instruments developed more quickly than the wind instruments, permitting them to play in any tonality, having intonation as precise as the performer's ear and technique permitted, and they could play long, sustained passages. Gradually wind instruments were added to the orchestra as they evolved and were needed, but to this day, a string orchestra has a unity of timbre and a beauty of tone that is unmatched by mixed ensembles. The same holds true for smaller groups of strings, namely string trios, quartets and quintets.

ADAGIO FOR STRINGS

by Samuel Barber

In the summer of 1935, the young American composer Samuel Barber was awarded the Prix de Rome. Only two of his major compositions had at that time been publicly performed. At twenty-five, he was essentially an unknown composer.

The Prix de Rome allowed the recipient to study at the American Academy in Rome, and offered $2500 for expenses and free living quarters. Toward the end of August, Barber sailed for Italy. He was pleased with the studio provided for him at the Academy — the old Villa Auerelia — but disliked his room in an apartment building. He wrote to a friend:

> "Do you know that I have not unpacked my trunk ... because I do not wish to feel at home in this room? My half-full trunk stands open, in complete disorder, the scandal of the Academy. And I shall not unpack it! I will never call this room mine! Not so for my studio which is full of charm, and I love the garden, the pines by moonlight, Rome in the distance, the yellow stone stairs."[1]

During the two years that Barber was at the Academy, he spent as much time away from Rome as he could. In the spring of 1936 he left with a friend of his, fellow-composer Gian-Carlo Menotti, for a trip northward to Lugano and Salzburg. They rented a little lodge in the woods

[1] Letter quoted in Nathan Broder's "Samuel Barber" (New York: G. Schirmer, Inc., 1954)

at St. Wolfgang, a few miles from Salzburg. It was a game warden's cottage which the two rented for $100 for the whole summer. This fee included the services of the warden's wife who did all the cooking and housekeeping.

The lodge was located at the foot of a mountain; a stream ran past the cottage. Amidst such rustic beauty Barber was inspired. He quickly composed one of his finest choral works, "Let Down the Bars, O Death," and a string quartet.

Later in the summer, the Italian-American conductor, Arturo Toscanini, asked Barber to show him some of his shorter compositions with the idea in mind that perhaps he could find something for use on his broadcasts with the NBC Symphony the following season. Barber thereupon set to work scoring the slow movement, an "Adagio," from his string quartet for string orchestra. Toscanini liked this new "Adagio for Strings" and broadcast it nationwide with his orchestra on November 5th, 1938. He later scheduled it for his South American concerts when he toured with his orchestra, the only work he performed by an American composer. Since then, the work has enjoyed wide popularity.

"Molto adagio espressivo cantando" — "Very slow, with song-like expression" — is the marking at the beginning of the score. In B-flat minor, the original meter signature is 4/2, but there are measures marked 5/2, 6/2 and 3/2. Although the tempo is slow and the melody flowing, the basic rhythm and pulse are never lost.

The "Adagio for Strings," some seven and a half minutes in length, is based entirely on one melodic idea which is then treated in somewhat contrapuntal manner.

The melodic idea, Example 1, consists of three phrases, the first and third being identical except for their closing. Example 1 is heard immediately over sustained chords played by divided second violins (two parts), violas, divided cellos (two parts) and double basses.

Example 1*

The violas enter on a different pitch level, in imitation. They play the violin melody, starting with Example 1, with a few minor variants.

A brief dialogue between violins and violas, in contrapuntal style, follows.

The cellos, now in unison, take up the theme, Example 1. The music increases in intensity during the cello statement.

In counterpoint to the cellos, the first violins play the first phrase of the theme; the second violins, now in unison, repeat the first phrase to a countermelody in the first violins. The first phrase is heard a third time, the first violins playing it an octave higher in pitch than the second violins. This leads to a forceful and dramatic climax on an F-flat major chord.

A pause follows. There are some soft, sustained chords.

The first violins and violas, now in unison, make a final statement of the theme, Example 1, in altered form. The music dies away at the end in soft, sustained chords, coming to rest on a final chord of F major.

Samuel Barber

(March 9, 1910 -   )

Samuel Barber was born in a century-old home in the quiet Pennsylvania community of West Chester. His father was a successful doctor who was anxious for his son to follow in his footsteps in the medical profession. The elder Barber had little interest in music, although his wife — Samuel's mother — was a pianist and her sister, Louis Homer, was a leading contralto at the Metropolitan Opera House.

Samuel started taking piano lessons when he was six and first tried his hand at composition a year later. One of his first attempts at opera (he was ten at the time) was the composition of one act of an opera called "The Rose Tree" to a script by the Barber's Irish cook.

Barber attended the Curtis Institute of Music in Philadelphia after graduation from high school. He became their first student to major in three fields: piano, composition and voice. At the Institute he became acquainted with an Italian student (who later became a United States citizen) Gian-Carlo Menotti with whom he formed a life-long friendship.

For his talents in composition, Barber received many prizes and awards. The first was the $1200 Bearns Prize which enabled him to go to Salzburg, Austria, to study. Money from his family allowed him to spend the summer of 1929 and 1930 in Italy with the family of his friend Menotti. Next came a $1500 Pulitzer Traveling Scholarship, and then the Prix de Rome.

Barber is best known for two operas, "Vanessa" and "Anthony and Cleopatra," both performed at the Metropolitan Opera, and for two symphonic works, his Symphony No. 1 and his "Essay for Orchestra."

LYRIC   SUITE

by Alban Berg

Alban Berg was a shy, quiet man who never appeared on the concert stage as a conductor or performer. Always plagued with poor health, he was happiest when he could retreat to a small mountain lodge, away from his native city of Vienna.

Berg's "Lyric Suite," composed in 1926, is considered one of the finest examples of twentieth-century chamber music. It took Berg more than a year to complete the score, for he was a perfectionist who labored slowly and somewhat painstakingly.

The "Lyric Suite" was composed for two violins, viola and cello; yet Berg avoided calling this work a string quartet. He realized that most string quartets are formal and symphonic in nature, whereas his work was to be more songlike and dramatic.

The six movements of Berg's "Lyric Suite" are not dances (as in Baroque suites) but intense, highly dramatic, related movements. They seem to depict the extremes of joy and sadness, and, at times, express a kind of insanity. Screeching tones, harsh chords, swoops and glides and rasping noises become a part of this very expressive music.

Berg presents us with a wide spectrum of color, as he exploits the highest and lowest range of the strings. The highest sounds are produced through harmonics, resulting by lightly touching a string at certain points on the fingerboard. The composer calls for a variety of string effects, including pizzicato, am Frosch (playing at the low end of the bow), flautando (bowing near the fingerboard with the point of the bow to produce a flute-like tone), echo and tremolo.

Berg uses a wide dynamic range, from ppp to fff, and he often asks for sudden contrasts such as ffp and fp. All these devices contribute to the broad sweep and emotional intensity of the music.

First Movement: Allegretto gioviale

In the first movement of the "Lyric Suite," marked "Allegretto gioviale" (moderately quick and jovial), Berg uses the twelve-tone technique. This music avoids a sense of tonality (hence is sometimes called atonal). Instead, the composer has selected a sequence of all the twelve half-tones within the span of an octave. All melodies and chords are derived from this (rather than from a major or minor scale). This arbitrary sequence of half-tones is known as a row. It can be transposed (started on a different pitch level), or inverted (turned upside down). To avoid a sense of tonality, ordinarily no member of the row can be repeated until all the other tones in the row have been employed either in the melodic line or in the accompanying harmony.

In the second measure, Berg reveals the row which is the basis for the first movement:

Example 1*

The introductory measure of this movement compacts into three chords all twelve tones of the row. It ends with a dissonant chord. Then follows the rhythmical form of the row, Example 1, in the first violin, a theme whose "joviality" is obvious.

In the next three measures the theme disappears. The cello continues the theme, then violin and cello play the figure G-flat - F - E (10, 1 and 2 of the row). In the seventh measure, the rhythm of the main theme, Example 1, is begun on E-flat and continues in its regular series, one after another; this is canonically imitated in the viola and second violin.

A bridge passage leads to the introduction of the second subject, marked <u>Poco più tranquillo</u> — "a little more tranquil" — Example 2. This theme is made up of 8, 9, 11 and 12 of the row, the missing 10 (A-flat) being taken by the viola. Against the theme of Example 2, the other tones of the row appear in harmony in the other voices.

Example 2

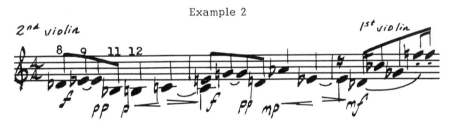

A closing theme of three measures brings the first section of this movement to a close, an upward staccato sweep from a low C-natural in the cello to a very high C-sharp in the first violin.

A recapitulation-development follows, a section in which the melodic material is repeated, but in a new manner developed from its earlier statement.

The pitches of Example 1 are repeated, but the octave in which some of them appear changes. Because the rhythm is also different, it is difficult to hear this melody as the first subject.

Again the tempo accelerates to bring the first subject to a conclusion. After a brief retard, alternating pizzicato and legato fragments indicate the bridge to the second theme, Example 2. The second theme, again marked "tranquil," appears in the upper register of the violin.

The Coda closes with the tone row. This time, however, the row appears not as a melodic idea, but as a harmonic cadence on a B-major chord:

Example 3

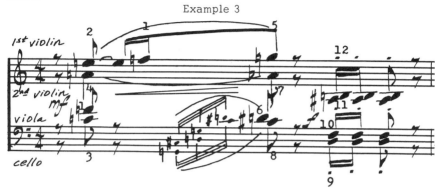

<u>Twelve-tone System</u> (known also as <u>Dodecaphonic Music</u>) : About 1921 the composer Arnold Schoenberg, after a period of experimentation in writing music without tonality (in other words, <u>atonal</u> music), devised a system which embodied all twelve tones of the chromatic scale. In it, the basis of both melodies and chords of a composition is an arrangement of the twelve notes of a chromatic scale in a particular order called a <u>tone row</u>. This series is always used complete, but may be transposed to any of the other positions, inverted, reversed (known as <u>retrograde</u>), or both reversed and inverted. It therefore has 48 forms, and, in addition, any tone of the series may be used in any octave, thus changing the contour of the row.

Schoenberg was followed in his use of this system by two fellow Austrians, his pupils Anton Webern and Alban Berg. Many other composers followed, including Ernst Krenek, and some later works of Igor Stravinsky.

Alban Berg

(February 9, 1885 – December 24, 1935)

Alban Berg was one of four children reared in a Roman Catholic home. His father was a bookseller and a dealer in religious articles; his mother was a daughter of the Court jewler and a talented painter and amateur musician.

Berg stated in a letter written later in life that, "before I started to compose I wanted to be a poet ... and, further back still, as a child I used to paint and draw, prompted by a certain manual skill which I mistook for talent."

The youth first turned to composition when he was fourteen, but the death of his father a year later destroyed the boy's hopes of successfully developing those talents in financial security. In the same year as his father's passing, Alban had his first attack of asthma. It was his poor health, along with a concentrated effort to compose about seventy songs and duets, that caused him to neglect his school work. When he failed to pass the examination at the end of the 1903 school year — and being frustrated in a youthful romance — he thought of suicide.

The following year he successfully passed the examination and graduated. He then became an accountant in a government office. Fortunately for Alban, his brother Charles saw an advertisement in the newspaper stating that Arnold Schoenberg was a teacher of composition. Charles

BMI Archives.

showed Schoenberg some of Alban's youthful creations; Schoenberg was impressed and offered to teach the nineteen-year-old lad free of charge.

By 1906 Berg inherited enough money to enable him to leave his government post and devote his time and talent exclusively to music. Today he is best remembered for his two operas, "Wozzeck" and "Lulu" (left incomplete at the time of his death), his Violin Concerto, the "Lyric Suite" and his "Three Orchestral Pieces."

"TROUT" QUINTET

by Franz Schubert

During the summer of 1819, Franz Schubert went to visit some friends in Steyr, one of the most beautiful little towns in Austria. It is located at the junction of the Enns and Steyr Rivers and its central market square with a stately fountain dates from the Middle Ages. The old stone house in which the composer stayed was located on this old market square and itself dated from the fifteenth century. Schubert wrote home to his brother: "Steyr is wonderful! The town is charming and the country around it unbelievably magnificent."

Schubert became acquainted in Steyr with an amateur cellist by the name of Sylvester Paumgartner. He was a wealthy bachelor who lived in a very large house with a music room on the first floor in which he held private musical parties, and a large music salon on the second floor where mid-day concerts and other musical activities took place. He asked Schubert to write a quintet for him using a violin, viola, cello, bass viol and piano. He suggested to the composer that his song, "The Trout," was one of his favorites; he hoped that perhaps Schubert could incorporate in the quintet a Theme with Variations movement based on this melody.

Schubert complied with Paumgartner's wishes and wrote a five movement Quintet, making the fourth movement a Theme with Variations based on the melody of his earlier song. He did not complete the quintet while he was in Steyr and had to post the music back to Paumgartner after he finished it in Vienna. The composition then completely disappeared until ten years later when Schubert's brother sold it to Josef Czerny, a music publisher in Vienna, who said:

> "This Quintet, having already been performed in several circles at my request, and declared to be a masterpiece by all the musicians present on each occasion, I think it is my duty to draw the public's attention to this latest work by the unforgettable composer ... "

But by that time Schubert was beyond such wonderful praise; he had been dead for a year.

Fourth Movement: Theme with Variations

The "Theme," derived from Schubert's song "The Trout," is in binary form. The first part is eight measures in length and is repeated. (It begins as in Example 1.) The second part (Example 2) is twelve measures in length and is not repeated. The Theme is presented by the violin; the accompaniment, without piano, is written in a rather simple harmonic style.

Example 1

Example 2

146

Variation 1

In the first Variation, the Theme appears in the piano with some embellishments (decorations in the melodic line). The violin is heard with figurations above the melody which are, in turn, echoed by the cello. The viola keeps up a steady pattern of triplet figures while a pizzicato part for the bass viol punctuates the accompaniment.

Example 3

Variation 2

The viola states the Theme while the violin plays a prominent countermelody, Example 4.

Example 4

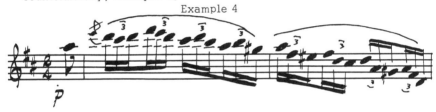

Variation 3

The cello and bass viol play the Theme in octaves. Simple staccato chords for the violin and viola accompany it; at the same time, the piano plays a sparkling countermelody, Example 5.

Example 5

Variation 4

In the fourth variation, the Theme is more implied than stated. The violin (Example 6), along with the viola and piano, play the harmony implied in the Theme; the mind of the listener actually supplies the original Theme. A busy countermelody in triplet figures appears in the cello and bass viol.

This variation opens in the minor mode and corresponds in atmosphere to the third and sinister stanza of the song in which the singer states,

> "At last the crafty angler
> As time went by
> Made that clear brooklet
> Oh, so muddy.
>
> At that I gave a cry!
> The rod and line were shaken.
> The trout, oh, the trout
> Was firmly caught!"

The Variation moves on to the relative major tonality, but by the end of the Variation, a return is made to the minor mode.

Example 6

Variation 5

The cello now takes up the Theme, Example 7, now altered chromatically.

Example 7

Allegretto

The Theme is now restated by the violin, accompanied in the first eight measures only by the piano. The piano accompaniment is similar to the piano accompaniment of the original song.

The cello makes the repeat of the first part of the Theme, Example 1. The other bowed strings (violin, viola and bass viol) accompany; the piano is not heard.

Once again the violin takes up the Theme, this time its second part, Example 2; only the piano accompanies it.

The second part of the Theme, Example 2, is now repeated by the cello, accompanied by bowed strings. Before this restatement is finished, the violin joins the cello in it and the piano joins the other strings in the accompaniment.

The brief Coda is based on a piano figure; it appears first in the piano, finally in the cello.

Franz Schubert

(January 31, 1797 – November 19, 1828)

For a biographical sketch, see page 134.

Chapter XIII

ELECTRONIC MUSIC

The world of electronic music is one full of fascinating, interesting sounds. Sometimes it suggests fantastic scenes which seem to come right out of the best science fiction novels. At other times, listeners become intriqued by the strange sounds it can produce, the unusual scale patterns it can develop, the extremely complicated polyrhythms that can evolve. You may find your curiosity aroused just by the word "electronic" itself!

What is electronic music? Actually there are two principal kinds. The first is called musique concrète; it is music based on natural sounds — dripping water, the sound of a human voice, the noise of a train. Such sounds are then changed and modified by electronic means until the desired composition results. This is called musique concrète — "concrete music" — because the composer is working directly or "concretely" with the sound while he changes or modifies it. This is in contrast to the traditional composer who deals only in abstract or non-concrete musical symbols — notes, rests, key and time signatures, etc. — which he puts on paper, and which do not become actual sounds or music until much later when performers actually play it.

The second type is called electronic music. True electronic music is music in which the original sound is synthesized or produced by an electrical device or gadget.

The first experiments in electronic music began as early as 1906 in Holyoke, Massachusetts, with the experiments of Dr. Thaddeus Cahill and his 200-ton dynamophone, the world's largest musical instrument. It wasn't until the tape recorder was fully developed around 1940, however, that musique concrète became possible.

The development of plastic tape recording began in 1927 with experiments by Pleumer, a German scientist who lived in Dresden. He tried coating plastic tape with iron oxide, commonly known as rust. In 1931 a German firm, A.E.G., began the development of a machine to use this coated tape of cellulose acetate. They called their tape recorder a magnetophone. By 1938, this machine — unknown outside Nazi Germany — was suitable for broadcasting.

After its development, most people thought of the tape recorder as just another type of phonograph for preserving the sound of a live performance. A few composers, however, started to think of it as a creative tool, a

machine on which music could actually be created. The first tape compositions were publically performed in France in 1950. A year later an electronic music laboratory was established in the broadcasting studio of Radio Cologne in Germany.

By 1952, the first tape music was heard in the United States. It was performed at the McMillan Theater on the Columbia University campus in New York. Vladimir Ussachevsky, a Russian-American who was teaching at Columbia at the time, was the composer. He created his compositions on an Ampex tape recorder given the University for the purpose of recording student concerts. The chairman of Columbia's composition faculty, Otto Luening, was fascinated by the sound of this new music. He invited Ussachevsky to present his experiments at the 1952 Bennington Composers Conference in Vermont. Luening reported that after the demonstration, a number of composers had solemnly congratulated him, saying: "This is it," — it meaning the music of the future.

Word was soon passed around about this experiment, and Ussachevsky and Luening were invited to produce a group of pieces for a program to be held at New York's Museum of Modern Art. The concert took place on October 28, 1952. A New York newspaper reported the next day that it had been a long time in coming, but music and the machine were finally wed.

A year later the young German composer, Karlheinz Stockhausen, created a piece of music entirely by electronic means. Instead of starting with the sound of a piano or flute or voice, he used a sound created electrically. He used what electronic engineers call an oscillator or tone generator. This device creates a pattern of regular electronic vibrations or oscillations, which — when fed into a loudspeaker system — produce musical pitch.

Before long, electronic engineers, in cooperation with young composers, were building machines which included all kinds of electronic devices for creating tone (sine-wave generators, white-noise generators, etc.) and for modifying it (filters, ring modulators, echo reverberation units, etc.) They called their new machines synthesizers. RCA's Mark II synthesizer was the first, but today those manufactured by Moog, Buchla and Electrocomp are better known.

DRIPSODY

by Hugh Le Caine

Hugh Le Caine, a Canadian scientist-engineer, composed "Dripsody" — subtitled "An Etude for Variable Speed Recorder" — in 1955 while developing instruments for electronic music studios.

There is a single sound source in "Dripsody," that of the fall of a single drop of water, hence this is an example of musique concrète since the sound source is an actual occurrence in nature.

The original tape recording of the single drop of water was approximately a half inch in length! It was copied at various speeds to produce sounds having fundamental frequencies from 45 cycles per second to 8000 cycles per second.

The rhythmic figures which imitate the rhythms of dripping water were written down in musical notation, and set up on tape by splicing together prints of the proper pitch. The tapes thus obtained were combined in a variety of ways.

"Dripsody," which lasts less than two minutes, took hundreds of hours of laboratory time for its creation. The work of splicing tape, reproducing sounds at various speeds, and so on, is an extremely laborious job. This is part of the role of the composer of musique concrète, for after he has the mental image of the piece he wishes to create, countless hours of tedious laboratory work are necessary to bring the composition to fruition.

Hugh Le Caine

1914 –   )

Hugh Le Caine was born in Port Arthur, Ontario (Canada) in 1914. He received a Bachelor of Science degree in physics from Queens University in Kingston, Ontario, in 1938 and his Master's degree at the same institution a year later. In 1940 he joined the staff of the National Research

Council of Canada and worked on the development of r a d a r components throughout the years of World War II.

From 1948 to 1952 Le Caine stud‑ied at the University of Birmingham in England on a National Research grant, a n d obtained h i s doctor's degree in physics.

On his return to the National Re‑search Council, he made a study of the application of technical know‑ledge — particularly in electronics — to methods of making music, old and new. The most interesting ap‑plications proved to be t h e new music‑making methods discovered by t h e musique c o n c r e t e group o f France in 1938.

Dr. Le Caine provided the techni‑cal guidance that helped establish the Electronic Music Studio at the University of Toronto early in the 1950s. It was the first such studio in Canada, and the second on the North American continent! Since

opening its doors for the first time, the EMS, as it is called, has grown from a small experimental studio with a minimum of equipment to a fully equipped sound studio, where not only experimentation with new sound is carried out, but where young composers can be and are being trained to work in this new medium of sound and music.

It was while making this installation that scientist Le Caine began to experiment with the equipment and became composer Le Caine!

EVOLUTIONS

by Henk Badings

"Evolutions" is a ballet suite made up of short electronic pieces whose elements demonstrate both contrast and unity. This makes the resulting work well suited to serve the purposes of the dance. As in most of Badings' works, the greatest merit lies in its clearly defined and well‑balanced form. In general, he uses forms which are descended from classical models, although he is never the slave of these models.

This ballet suite was composed in 1958, and first performed in the same year by the Hanover Opera Ballet in Germany. One of the most interesting things about this ballet music is the fact that its source sound is electronically produced and then modified or changed by other electronic devices, and all put together on tape. Reproduced over loudspeakers in the opera houses where it has been made to compete with traditional ballet music played by symphony orchestras (as has been the case in Rome and Vienna), it has been highly acclaimed by the audiences.

In Vienna, for example, it was performed at the Vienna State Opera House, a place rich in tradition. The discussions beforehand in the Viennese press left no doubt as to the expectations: "desecration of the sacred halls." The evening of March 24, 1959, passed otherwise. Press and public voted in favor of electronic music! One critic wrote in his paper the following day: "This fantastic-sounding and fantastically danced vision of the future received, to the surprise of all, tempestuous applause from the conservative Viennese opera audience, and was undoubtedly the most important event of this season at the Vienna State Opera."

The entire ballet suite, "Evolutions," was created at the studio of the Philips physics laboratory at Eindhoven, The Netherlands. The sound sources were varied: sine-wave generators, a sawtooth generator, a white-noise generator and pulse generators. These electronic sounds were modified by modulators, filters and reverberation apparatus.

There are six movements to the complete ballet: Overture, Air, Ragtime, Intermezzo, Waltz and Finale.

The Air, a "pas de deux," is lyrical and elegiac. The Ragtime is a fantasy on the well-known rhythm of $3 + 2 + 3$ beats, with ecstatic "breaks" of electronic percussion, a lyrical melody and a dramatic closing episode.

The meaning the original choreographer, Yvonne Georgi, heard in "Evolutions" and wanted to express through the medium of the dance was modern man's agony in a technical world: his restlessness, his striving, his near-grotesque wavering between hope and despair.

Henk Badings

(January 17, 1907 -   )

Henk Badings was born at Bandung, Java, on January 17, 1907. Growing up in The Netherlands, he took violin lessons and began to compose at an early age. The career for which he trained, however, was that of mining engineer. He took his degree with honors at the Technical University of Delft, The Netherlands, in 1931. After this he spent four years as assistant at the university's department of paleontology and historical geology.

In the meantime he took some lessons in composition from Willem Pijper, but Badings had already completed his Symphony No. 1 by the time the lessons started. Thus he may be described as essentially a self-taught composer. The Symphony No. 1 was most successful, and encouraged him to follow with others. His Symphony No. 3 gained for him an international reputation.

Badings soon began to devote all his energies to music. He has written a large number of works of almost every kind: concertos, piano sonatas, chamber music, songs, choral works, operas (including a radio opera, "Orestes," which won the Italia Prize in 1945), oratorios, ballets and incidental music.

DISCOGRAPHY

CHAPTER   I

"Ironsides" by Quincy Jones
     Jones, Richardson, Hubbard, Lawes
     A & M 3037

"The Godfather" by Nino Rota
     Original Soundtrack
     Paramount 1003

CHAPTER   II

"Rodeo" by Aaron Copland
     New York Philharmonic, Leonard Bernstein
     Columbia MS 6175

"Three Places in New England" by Charles Ives
     Philadelphia Orchestra, Eugene Ormandy
     Columbia MS 7015

CHAPTER   III

"España" by Emmanuel Chabrier
     New York Philharmonic, Leonard Bernstein
     Columbia MS 6786

"In the Steppes of Central Asia" by Alexander Borodin
     Philadelphia Orchestra, Eugene Ormandy
     Columbia MS 6875

"Roman Carnival Overture" by Hector Berlioz
     Suisse Romande, Ernst Ansermet
     London 2101

155

CHAPTER   IV

"An American in Paris" by George Gershwin
New York Philharmonic, Leonard Bernstein
Columbia MS 6091

"Platero y Yo" by Mario Castelnuovo-Tedesco
Andrés Segovia, guitar
Decca DL 10054

Polonaise in A-flat by Frédéric Chopin
Artur Rubinstein, piano
RCA/Victor LSC 7037

CHAPTER   V

"Rumanian Folk Dances" by Béla Bartók
Suisse Romande, Ernst Ansermet
London 6407

"Age of Gold" by Dmitri Shostakovich
Bolshoi Theater Orchestra, M. Shostakovich
Melodia/Angel S-40062

Dances from "The Bartered Bride" by Bedřich Smetana
Berlin Philharmonic, Herbert von Karajan
Deutsche Grammophon 2530244

CHAPTER   VI

"Jesus Christ Superstar" by Andrew Lloyd Webber
Original (London) Cast Album
Decca 71503

"Passio et mors domini nostri Jesu Christi secundum Lucam" by
Krzysztof Penderecki
Cracow Philharmonic, Henryk Czyz

Cantata No. 147 by Johann Sebastian Bach
King's College Choir, Willcocks
Angel S-36804

CHAPTER   VII

"Nocturnes" by Claude Debussy
London Symphony, Pierre Monteux
London 6248

"The Pines of Rome" by Ottorino Respighi
Chicago Symphony, Fritz Reiner
RCA/Victor 2436

Symphony No. 6 by Ludwig van Beethoven
Chicago Symphony, Fritz Reiner
RCA/Victor LSC 2614

CHAPTER   VIII

"Afro-American Symphony" by William Grant Still
Royal Philharmonic, Karl Krueger
Society for Preservation of American Musical Heritage MIA 118

"English Folk Song Suite" by Ralph Vaughan Williams
London Symphony, Sir Adrian Boult
Angel S-36799

"Academic Festival Overture" by Johannes Brahms
Cleveland Orchestra, George Szell
Columbia MS 6965

CHAPTER   IX

"St. Louis Blues" by W. C. Handy
(1) W. C. Handy, trumpet; and (2) Louis Armstrong, trumpet
Special Commemorative Album, "Father of the Blues"
c/o Florence Chamber of Commerce, Florence, Ala. 35630

"Miles" by Miles Davis
Davis, Adderley, Coltrane, Garland, Chambers, "Philly" Jones
Columbia CS 8633

CHAPTER   X

Overture to "Die Meistersinger von Nürnberg" by Richard Wagner
Berlin Philharmonic, Rafael Kubelik
Deutsche Grammophon 136228

"Swan Lake" by Peter Ilyitch Tchaikovsky
Philadelphia Orchestra, Eugene Ormandy
Columbia MS 6807

CHAPTER   XI

"Bachianas Brasileiras No. 5" by Heitor Villa-Lobos
Davrath; New York Philharmonic, Leonard Bernstein
Columbia MS 6514

"Liebeslieder Walzer" by Johannes Brahms
Valente, Kleinman, Conner, Singher w/Serkin, Fleisher
Columbia MS 6236

"The Trout" by Franz Schubert
Elisabeth Schumann, soprano; George Reeves, piano
Angel COLH 130

CHAPTER   XII

"Adagio for Strings" by Samuel Barber
Philadelphia Orchestra, Eugene Ormandy
Columbia MS 6224

"Lyric Suite" by Alban Berg
Juilliard Quartet
RCA/Victor LSC 2531

"Trout" Quintet by Franz Schubert
H. Menuhin, Amadeus Quartet
Angel S-35777

CHAPTER   XIII

"Dripsody" by Hugh Le Caine
Folkways 33436

"Evolutions" by Henk Badings
Philips 835 056 AY

INDEX